# Business Processes

A Database Perspective

# Synthesis Lectures on Data Management

Editor
**M. Tamer Özsu,** *University of Waterloo*

Synthesis Lectures on Data Management is edited by Tamer Özsu of the University of Waterloo. The series will publish 50- to 125 page publications on topics pertaining to data management. The scope will largely follow the purview of premier information and computer science conferences, such as ACM SIGMOD, VLDB, ICDE, PODS, ICDT, and ACM KDD. Potential topics include, but not are limited to: query languages, database system architectures, transaction management, data warehousing, XML and databases, data stream systems, wide scale data distribution, multimedia data management, data mining, and related subjects.

Business Processes: A Database Perspective
Daniel Deutch and Tova Milo
2012

Data Protection from Insider Threats
Elisa Bertino
2012

Deep Web Query Interface Understanding and Integration
Eduard C. Dragut, Weiyi Meng, and Clement T. Yu
2012

P2P Techniques for Decentralized Applications
Esther Pacitti, Reza Akbarinia, and Manal El-Dick
2012

Query Answer Authentication
HweeHwa Pang and Kian-Lee Tan
2012

Declarative Networking
Boon Thau Loo and Wenchao Zhou
2012

Business Processes: A Database Perspective

Daniel Deutch and Tova Milo


ISBN: 978-3-031-00763-7     paperback
ISBN: 978-3-031-01891-6     ebook


DOI 10.1007/978-3-031-01891-6


A Publication in the Springer series
*SYNTHESIS LECTURES ON DATA MANAGEMENT*

Lecture #27
Series Editor: M. Tamer Özsu, *University of Waterloo*
Series ISSN
Synthesis Lectures on Data Management
Print 2153-5418   Electronic 2153-5426

# Business Processes

## A Database Perspective

Daniel Deutch
Ben Gurion University

Tova Milo
Tel Aviv University

*SYNTHESIS LECTURES ON DATA MANAGEMENT #27*

## ABSTRACT

While classic data management focuses on the data itself, research on Business Processes also considers the *context* in which this data is generated and manipulated, namely the processes, users, and goals that this data serves. This provides the analysts a better perspective of the organizational needs centered around the data. As such, this research is of fundamental importance.

Much of the success of database systems in the last decade is due to the beauty and elegance of the relational model and its declarative query languages, combined with a rich spectrum of underlying evaluation and optimization techniques, and efficient implementations. Much like the case for traditional database research, elegant modeling and rich underlying technology are likely to be highly beneficiary for the Business Process owners and their users; both can benefit from easy formulation and analysis of the processes. While there have been many important advances in this research in recent years, there is still much to be desired: specifically, there have been many works that focus on the processes behavior (flow), and many that focus on its data, but only very few works have dealt with both the state-of-the-art in a database approach to Business Process modeling and analysis, the progress towards a holistic flow-and-data framework for these tasks, and highlight the current gaps and research directions.

## KEYWORDS

business processes, data models, query languages, process analysis

# Contents

# Acknowledgments

The authors would like to thank all of their collaborators and friends who (directly or indirectly) contributed to the making of this book, including in particular: Serge Abiteboul, Yael Amsterdamer, Zhuowei Bao, Catriel Beeri, Rubi Boim, Susan Davidson, Anat Eyal, Ohad Greenshpan, H. V. Jagadish, Christoph Koch, Alon Pilberg, Neoklis Polyzotis, Sudeepa Roy, Julia Stoyanovich, Pierre Senellart, Val Tannen, Victor Vianu, and Tom Yam.

Daniel Deutch's work is partially supported by the Israeli Ministry of Science and the Binational (US-Israel) Science Foundation.

Tova Milo's work is partially supported by the Israeli Science Foundation, the Binational (US-Israel) Science Foundation, the Israeli Ministry of Science, and the European Research Council under the European Community's 7th Framework Programme (FP7/2007-2013) / ERC grant MoDaS, grant agreement 291071.

Last but not least, we wish to thank our families. Tova Milo thanks her husband, Amir Milo, and her children, Eran and Yuval Milo, for their constant support (and tolerance). Daniel Deutch thanks Yael and his parents, Orna and Miguel, for all their care and support.

Daniel Deutch and Tova Milo
July 2012

CHAPTER 1

# Introduction

Recent years have seen a shift in data management research. While research on stand-alone database management continues to be foundational, increasing attention is directed towards the *context* in which this data are generated and manipulated, namely *the processes, users, and goals* that this data serves. In a nutshell, this is what research on *business processes* (BP for short) is all about.

A business process consists of a group of business activities undertaken by one or more organizations in pursuit of some particular goal. Such business processes describe the operational logic of applications, including the possible *application flow* and the *data* that are manipulated by it. Research in this direction involves marrying ideas and concepts from database management, with ideas from workflow and process flow management, that previously have been mostly studied separately. This combined flow-and-data management in business processes is the focus of this book. We note that we use here the term "business processes" in a very broad sense and the problems and solutions that we will consider are applicable to many other contexts that involve data and flow, such as scientific workflows, Web applications and services, e-government and electronic patient records.

Consider, for example, an online travel agency that suggests a variety of possible reservations of flights, hotels and car rental, and combinations thereof. Research that focuses only on the travel agency underlying data, its storage and manipulation (perhaps in a distributed setting, or even in the cloud) can tell us how to design the database, and how to query it in an optimal way. However, in the broader perspective of the company, its database is only a tool that is used in the company *Business Process*, which, to the company, is itself of no less interest than the data. For instance, the company may provide an online interface for reserving trips. In this case, the interaction with the database may be initiated by a reservation requested by an online user; the process in charge of processing of this reservation will query the database to find suitable matches, that in turn will be presented to the user. If no match is available, the process may issue other queries on the database, possibly to recommend the user other alternatives. The user may then choose one of these options or ask for more recommendations, which will be computed using a refined query, and so on.

Knowledge about the operation of such a Business Process is thus of tremendous importance to both the company (or application) owners and their users. First, the process specification, and its possible executions flows, are themselves a valuable data; their analysis can be used by the application owners for detecting bugs or optimizing the process. For instance, in our online travel agency example, the company owners may wish to verify that a user can reserve a flight only after relaying her credit card details. Similarly, the application users may wish to infer the optimal ways of using the process, e.g., shortest (click-wise) navigation in the web-site to reserve a trip to a particular location, or one that leads to minimal cost, etc. Second, execution traces (logs) of business processes, detailing (parts of) the course of past execution, are another extremely valuable source of data. For example, logs analysis can reveal that customers who choose to search for combined flight and hotel deals, and then choose a flight of a particular airline, typically logout at this point without placing a reservation. This may suggest that the list of hotels suggested as combined deals with this particular airline are not attractive, or presented in an unattractive way; this may help to improve the application design or the suggested deals. A combined analysis that uses both the process specification and its execution traces may also be extremely valuable. This may allow, for instance, to obtain answers to questions such as "what other alternative actions could users whose airline request failed take, but didn't." This may be used to improve the user interface (UI) and make these options more apparent.

There have been many important advances in business processes modeling and analysis in recent years. There are several good models and techniques for capturing and analyzing the processes flow, and several good models and techniques for capturing and analyzing the data they manipulate. But there is still much to be desired. Specifically, we advocate in this book a particular, *declarative and holistic* approach for the modeling and analysis of business processes (both flow and data). Since this approach is rooted in the longstanding line of research of databases, we refer to it as *a database perspective*.

## 1.1    A DATABASE PERSPECTIVE TO BUSINESS PROCESSES

We observe that in the Business Process settings there is an inherent coupling of application *data* and *logic* (also referred to as *flow*): the flow affects the data and vice versa. This attracted the attention of database researchers (e.g., [Beeri et al., 2007; Deutsch et al., 2005; Fritz et al., 2009; Gaaloul and Godart, 2005; Grigori et al., 2004; Sayal et al., 2002]) that attempt to extend the good principles of data management (declarative specifications, optimization, etc.) to the broader perspective that includes not only the database itself but also the process surrounding it.

Specifically, much of the success of database systems in the last decade is due to the elegance of the relational model and declarative query languages, combined with a rich spectrum of underlying evaluation and optimization techniques, and efficient implementations. Similar accomplishments have recently being sought for in the context of business processes. What is desired here, in our opinion, is an equivalently elegant formal *model* and *declarative query languages*, that will allow easy formulation of analysis tasks, readability and seamless optimizations, while at the same time will be expressively rich and comprehensive enough to capture intricate processes flow, their manipulation of data, and complicated analysis tasks. This is a database perspective of the problem, drawing inspiration from the success of the relational model, towards the design of solutions for the modeling and analysis of business processes. In this book, we focus on this perspective, highlighting some of the main challenges in this area and (partial) successes in addressing them.

We next briefly review the main tasks that are required towards achieving this goal, in the order considered in this book.

*Personal Perspective*    In a series of works (see e.g., [Beeri et al., 2007; Deutch and Milo, 2008, 2009a,b; Deutch et al., 2010]), the authors of this book and collaborators have studied a particular model for business processes, its properties and the means for querying and analyzing it. While we also discuss other models, the focus of this book is on our particular model and techniques.

## 1.2    BOOK SCOPE AND ORGANIZATION

We next briefly outline the main subjects addressed in this book, according to their order of presentation. Each chapter is concluded with open questions and ideas for future work.

*Chapter 2: Modeling*    Similarly to the case of relational databases, the first challenge that should be addressed is one of *modeling*. One difficulty that arises when attempting an effective management of Business processes is the typical complexity of their representations. Business processes usually operate in a cross-organizational, distributed environment and the software implementing them is fairly complex. For instance, our travel agency company may interact in intricate ways with various airlines and hotel chains, with users who are placing orders, etc. Due to the complexity of the process and of its interactions (and much like the case of "classical" data management), effective Business Process management needs to rely on an abstract model for the Business Process.

Clearly, for business processes implemented in a language such as Java, their representation in such abstract models is not an easy task. Luckily, this gap is slowly being bridged by many *declarative standards* that facilitate the design, deployment, and execution of BPs. In particular, the recent Business Process Execution Language (BPEL) [bpel] standard, provides an XML-based language to describe the interface between the participants in a process, as well as the full operational logic of the process and its execution flow. The BPEL standard is relatively declarative, and it is much easier to abstract it further, to fit the model; there are also many graphical interfaces and editors that allow for a relatively simple, intuitive design of BPEL specifications.

Using the BPEL standard as our starting point, we designed an abstract model [Beeri et al., 2007] for Business Process specifications. A BP is modeled as a set of DAGs (Directed Acyclic Graphs), each consisting of activities (nodes), and links (edges) between them, that detail the execution order of the activities. Each activity is modeled by a pair of nodes, standing for its activation (start) point and its completion (end) point. Such a node pair is referred to as an *activation-completion* (abbr. act-comp) node. Each such DAG has a unique activity pair, with no incoming edges, standing as its *start* activity and a unique activity pair, with no outgoing edges, standing as its *end* activity. Activities that are not linked via a directed path are assumed to occur *in parallel*. The DAGs are linked through implementation relationships; the idea is that an activity *a* in one DAG is realized via the activities in another DAG. We call such an activity *compound* to differentiate it from *atomic* activities having no implementations. Compound activities may have multiple possible implementations, corresponding e.g., to different user choices, variable values, servers availability, etc. A unique DAG in the set, consisting of a single act-comp node, serves as the process *root*, standing for its starting point.

While each individual graph is a DAG, the implementation relation may induce cycles, e.g., for an activity $a$ in some DAG $G$, $G$ may appear as a possible implementation of $a$; alternatively, in some possible implementation $G'$ of the activity $a$, there may appear a compound activity $b$, having $G$ as a possible implementation, etc. In such cases we say that the BP is *recursive*.

Then, execution flows (abbr. EX-flows) are actual running instances of the Business Process representing the execution of its activities. An EX-flow may be abstractly viewed as a *nested DAG*: starting from the BP root, for each compound activity, exactly one of its implementations is chosen at runtime; then, for each compound activity node $n$ in the chosen implementation, one of its implementations is chosen etc. We model this by connecting, via new edges called *implementation* edges, the start and end nodes of the chosen implementation graph, to the activation and completion nodes of the corresponding compound activity node.

Note that for any given business process (BP) specification $s$, the size of a single EX-flow of $s$ may be unbounded if $s$ is recursive; in particular, this means that recursive BPs may have infinitely many possible EX-flows.

*Other models*    There is a long-standing line of research on modeling process flow; we next overview some of these works briefly and revisit them in more detail in Section 1.2.

The simplest model in this context is the well-known Finite State Machines [Hopcroft and Ullman, 1990]. While useful, Finite State Machines have a quite limited expressive power from a theoretical perspective and, furthermore, modeling real-life systems with them may be cumbersome, and require a large number of states. In particular, finite state models fail to capture the notion of code reuse via *functions*. In contrast, the model of *Hierarchical state machines* (HSMs) [Benedikt et al., 2001] allows to capture the counterpart of functions, in turn implemented by other HSMs, and so forth. This allows for some succinctness in expressing control flow, however it fails to allow unbounded *recursion*. In contrast, Recursive State Machines (RSMs) [Alur et al., 2005] extend HSMs by allowing the function calls to be (mutually) recursive.

An important aspect in the modeling of business processes is capturing the data manipulation and transformations performed by the process. Our model has been extended (as described in Chapter 2) to account for a limited modeling of data manipulation through the notion of *guarding formulas*. These are logical formulas that express equality relations between variables and data values. Another example for a (limited modeling of data) *scientific workflows*, i.e., processes that are executed by scientists and composed of modules. Each module performs some scientific task and the modules interact by passing data between them.

Additional lines of research focus on explicit modeling of the manipulated data, based on relational or semi-structured data models. In this context we will overview the model of Relational Transducers [Abiteboul et al., 1998] (and the follow-up work on ASM transducers [Spielmann, 2003]), that was shown to be very effective in capturing e-commerce applications. Essentially, the application is state is modeled via a relational database, and transitions are modeled via queries. A similar approach is taken in the works on Business Process artifacts [Abiteboul et al., 2011; Fritz et al., 2009; Hull and Su, 2005; Vianu, 2009]. The model focuses on the data received, generated and manipulated by the process (e.g., purchase orders, sales invoices, etc.). The data structures encapsulating this information are referred to in this context as *artifacts*. We also mention in this context the work on data-driven, interactive Web Applications [Bultan et al., 2006; Deutsch et al., 2005, 2006] where the state (database) is shared across various applications, each of which may read/write its contents. In the context of semi-structured data, we mention the Active XML model [ActiveXml] extends XML with Web Service calls, whose results are embedded back in the document, allowing to make additional calls etc. In a recent work, Abiteboul et al. [2011] suggest an artifacts model based on Active XML.

Chapter 2 overviews the above representation models for business processes, and focuses on details of our model.

*Chapter 3: Analysis*     Once a process model is given, it may be used for *process analysis*. The idea is that we are given a specification of the Business Process, and we wish to analyze its possible executions. For instance, for our travel agency example, we may be interested in verifying that no customer can make a reservation without paying; or that whenever such payment is processed, the system performs credit check before approving it. Alternatively, we may also be interested in computing the probability that some property holds in a random execution, e.g., what is the probability for a user to ask for a combination of particular airline and hotel. The results of such analysis are of interest to both the process owners and their users: the former may optimize their business processes, reduce operational costs, and ultimately increase competitiveness. The latter may allow users to make an optimal use of the process (e.g., find out what is the most popular way of ordering a trip to a particular location). Importantly, the results of such an analysis, that is aware not only of the company database, but also to the applications that manipulate it, can be very useful in improving the application and the service it suggests to customers.

Continuing with our database perspective, we consider a *query language* for the formulation of analysis tasks. We will review different formalisms that were proposed as query languages for this setting, including temporal logic [Emerson, 1990] and LTL-FO [Deutsch et al., 2005]. We then focus on our query language BPQL [Beeri et al., 2007]. Different facets of BPQL correspond to different analysis tasks. The basic construct that we will use in all different facets is referred to as *execution patterns* (EX-patterns), generalizing execution flows similarly to the way tree patterns, used in query languages for XML, generalize XML trees. A match of the query is captured via the notion of an *embedding*, which is a homomorphism from an execution pattern to an execution flow, respecting node labels and edge relation.

We then consider three types of queries:

1. *Selection queries*, that select all matches of qualifying EX-flows of a given specification with respect to the given EX-pattern.

2. *Projection queries*, where only parts (sub-flows) of the matched EX-flows are of interest.

3. *Boolean queries* that ask for the existence of such qualifying EX-flows (or for the probability of obtaining one in a random execution of the process.

As we will observe, the number of results of selection and projection queries may be extensively large (exponential in the size of the BP specification). Thus, rather than enumerating *all* results, we will focus on computing the *top-k* ones, based on a ranking function that is itself based on the weight function given as input (to be defined precisely in the sequel).

Our database perspective is reflected in the design of queries; our vision is to have a full-fledged query language, including additional features such as value-based joins.

*Chapter 4: Other Issues*   In Chapter 4 we provide a short overview of additional aspects that are relevant to business processes modeling and analysis. In particular, we focus on the following aspects:

**Design and Mining.** Before we can analyze the possible executions of a given BP, we need to derive its specification, i.e., an instance of the model. Graphical interfaces are very useful in promoting a high-level (formal) specification of a Business Process. Still, in many cases, the specification of the Business Process is partially or completely unknown. In such cases, the abstract model needs to be *mined* [Grigori et al., 2004; Sayal et al., 2002; van der Aalst et al., 2003] automatically, e.g., from a set of observed executions. We will review both facets (graphical design interfaces and mining techniques) of obtaining instances of process specifications.

**Analysis of Past Executions.** While in Chapter 3 we focus on the analysis of future executions, an additional facet of analysis is that of *past* executions. Execution logs detailing such past executions are of tremendous importance for companies, since they may reveal *patterns* in the behavior of the users (e.g., "users that order flights of a particular airline may also be interested in hotels of a particular chain"), may allow to identify run-time bugs that occurred, or a breach of the company policy etc. But the challenges are that typical repositories of such execution logs are of very large size, and that the patterns that are of interest are those that occur frequently but are not always known in advance. Consequently, various works considered data mining and OLAP (Online Analytical Process) techniques for querying logs repositories; but there are also some works that introduce query languages for execution traces. Continuing the analogy with Databases, what is required for specifying the analysis tasks is a *declarative query language*, supported by efficient *query evaluation mechanisms*. We briefly discuss in Chapter 4 the advances towards such a solution.

## INTENDED AUDIENCE

The book can serve as an introduction to business processes for database researchers, or as a textbook for an advanced graduate class.

## READERS' GUIDE

The rest of this book may be read in either of the following ways. Readers who are interested in a high-level overview of the models and analysis solutions may read Sections 2.1–2.3, 2.5, 3.1–3.2, 3.7 and Chapter 4. In contrast, other readers may be interested in an example of concrete definitions of a model (in particular, our model) as well as results pertaining to the model analysis. These are given in Section 2.4 and Sections 3.3–3.6, respectively. References to prior literature are provided for readers interested in exact details of other models mentioned in the book.

CHAPTER 2

# Modeling

Various models for business processes may be found in the literature. As process models in verification and model checking (see e.g., [Brand and Zafiropulo, 1983; Burch et al., 1992; Burkart and Steffen, 1992; Emerson, 1990; Kucera et al., 2006; Manna and Pnueli, 1992; Murata, 1989] and many others), these models differ in their expressive power, i.e., the sets of possible executions they can represent. We first provide an intuitive overview of some models, starting from simple ones and gradually considering models with greater expressive power. Then, in the second part of this chapter, we focus and elaborate on one particular such model, namely the BPQL model [Beeri et al., 2007].

## 2.1    FINITE STATE MACHINES

Perhaps the simplest model in this context is that of Finite State Machines (FSMs) [Hopcroft and Ullman, 1990]. When using FSMs to model BP specifications, the states correspond to the logical states of the application, and the transitions are dictated by (typically external) input.

**Example 2.1**    Consider the Finite State Machine depicted in Figure 2.1. The four states (Login, Advertise, Flight and Confirm) correspond to logical states of the application (waiting for user login, injecting advertisements to the screen, waiting for a user choice of flights, and confirmation). The transitions model possible logical flow between the states.

Finite State Machines have a quite limited expressive power from a theoretical perspective, and furthermore modeling real-life systems with them may be cumbersome, and require a large number of states. In particular, finite state models fail to capture the notion of code reuse via *functions*. In contrast, the model of *Hierarchical state machines*, presented next, allows for the capture of the counterpart of functions.

## 2.2    HIERARCHICAL STATE MACHINES

Hierarchical State Machines (HSMs) [Benedikt et al., 2001] allow definition of a hierarchy of Finite State Machines, in a way resembling "function calls." That is, an HSM consists of a set of state machines, and one state machine may "invoke" another, meaning that the control flow moves to the invoked machine; while the execution in this machine reaches an accepting state, the control

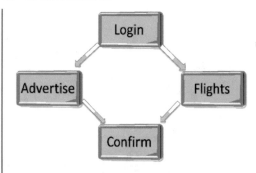

**Figure 2.1:** Finite State Machine.

returns to the invoking location[1]. The invocation may lead to one out of multiple possible machines (intuitively, corresponding to multiple possible implementations of the same function).

**Example 2.2**   Consider Figure 2.2. It provides a graphical representation of a (simplified) Hierarchical State Machine. The "bubbles" correspond to possible implementations of functions. In this example, the starting point for the application is the ChooseTravel activity, intuitively modeling e.g., the state of the application when a user reaches the agency's homepage. ChooseTravel has three possible implementations, intuitively corresponding to a search type chosen by the user: the first implementation (labeled F2) will be invoked if the user chooses to search only flights, the second (F3) if the user chooses to search for combined flights and hotels deals, and the third (F4) if the user chooses to search for combined deals of flights, hotels and cars. Each of these implementations is itself modeled by an HSM: note that some states (e.g., "Flights," "Hotels") model an additional function call, which has multiple possible implementations (corresponding here to the different possible choices of hotel chains, airlines, etc.).

The hierarchy of state machines gives conciseness to representation, but not more expressive power. In real-life processes, there is often the need to represent *recursion*. For instance, our specification should enable recursive invocations of the sub-process labeled F1, to allow for more and more choices. A more expressive model that accommodates (a restricted type of) recursion is that of *Recursive State Machine* (RSM), described next.

---

[1]We mention in this context that the notion of hierarchy, along with additional constructs, lies also at the core of StateCharts [Harel, 1987].

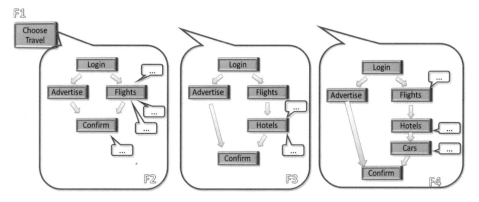

Figure 2.2: Hierarchical State Machine.

## 2.3    RECURSIVE STATE MACHINES

Recursive State Machines (RSMs) extend HSMs by allowing function calls to be (mutually) recursive. Recall that in an HSM, some of the states in any given state machine $M$ model function calls, and each of these functions are realized by another state machine $M'$, and so forth. In an RSM, the function called from a state of $M$ may be implemented by $M$ itself.

**Example 2.3**    Consider Figure 2.3, and note that now one of the possible implementations of "Confirm" is F1. This forms a mutual recursion between F1 and e.g., F2: a possible implementation of a node ("chooseTravel") in F1 is F2, and a possible implementation of a node in F2 is F1. In the application flow this allows to capture the notion of "reset," that is users may make choices, cancel them, and make other choices, an unbounded number of times.

There are multiple variants of RSMs, differing in the number of *entries* (initial states) and *exits* (final states) of the state machines. The class of RSMs where the state machines have multiple exits is strictly more expressive than the class of single exit recursive state machine [Alur et al., 2005].

*Choice vs. Parallelism*    There are different possible interpretations of *branching* in every Finite State Machine component of an HSM (or RSM). A first possible interpretation is that of *choice*, namely an execution is a path and for every point of branching exactly one branch is followed. Note that using this interpretation, there are two kinds of choices made in an execution: choice of branches as well as the choice of *implementations* for each of the functions invoked in the course of execution. Another possible interpretation of branching is as *parallelism*, namely both branches are taken and are assumed to be executed in parallel. Using this interpretation, a run is no longer a path but rather a *graph*. This allows for a more compact representation of possible runs, compared to trying all possible orderings of parallel branches.

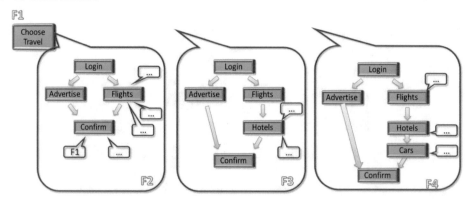

**Figure 2.3:** Recursive State Machine.

We note in this context that the set of possible runs obtained for a Recursive State Machine using the latter interpretation can also be captured by a *Context Free Graph Grammar* (CFGG) [Courcelle, 2004]. Intuitively, CFGGs resemble (string) context free grammars; instead of strings, the right-hand side of derivation rules in CFGGs are graphs, and non-terminals annotate nodes in these graphs. Upon derivation, nodes are replaced by sub-graphs that they derive and *connection relations* (that are part of the grammar specification) specify how these sub-graphs are connected to the graph in which the node resided in.

*Probabilistic Variants*   In the context of business processes, it is important to model the uncertainty that is inherent in the external effects that govern the executions. For example, the course of execution of our online travel agency Business Process depends on the choices of users, submitted through its web interface. The choices that users will make are unknown at the time of analyzing the process, but we may have some probabilistic knowledge of the behavior of users. The above mentioned models all have *probabilistic* counterparts, where the possible executions (derivations) are associated with probabilities of occurring in practice. The probabilistic counterpart of Finite State Machines is Markov Chains [Meyn and Tweedie, 1993], where every transition is associated with a probability of occurring in practice. These probabilities are assumed to be independent (the Markovian assumption is that the probability of taking a transition in a given state is independent on the previously made transitions), thus the probability of an execution is simply the multiplication of the probabilities along its transitions. Similar extensions were studied for probabilistic context free grammars (see e.g., [Lary and Young, 1990]), and Recursive Markov Chains (RMCs) [Etessami and Yannakakis, 2009] that are the counterpart of Recursive State Machines; in these extensions the Markovian property is also assumed.

While the independence assumption simplifies the models and allows for a more efficient analysis (See Section 2.3), it is in some cases unrealistic when modeling business processes. In particular, when the transitions are governed by external effects such as user choices, the state of the network, server response time, etc., it is unreasonable to assume their independence: for instance, users that choose a particular airline is more likely to later choose a hotel residing in a city which serves as a destination of these airlines flights. In the sequel, we present our model for *weighted* business processes, and show how it allows (in particular) to capture possibly dependent probabilistic distributions on choices that govern the Business Process execution.

*BPQL model*    So far we have provided only high-level, intuitive details on various models. In what follows we focus on a particular model for business processes (hereby after referred to as BPs for short), originally introduced in [Beeri et al., 2007]. This will allow us to explain some subtleties of the model definitions, and will also serve as concrete settings in which analysis tasks will be studied.

At a highlevel, the model of [Beeri et al., 2007] was shown to be equivalent in terms of expressivity to a restricted variant of RSMs (namely Single Entry Single Exit Recursive State Machines), but with the "parallelism" interpretation of branching as will be evident below. We next define the model formally.

## 2.4    BPQL MODEL

A BP specification encodes a set of activities and the order in which they may occur. The type of activities and their order depend on the business goals that the BP aims to achieve.

In the sequel, let $\mathcal{N}$ be a domain of graph nodes and $\mathcal{A}$ be a finite domain of activity names. A BP specification is represented by a set of DAGs that are linked through implementation relationships. The idea is that an activity $a$ in one DAG is realized by the activities in another DAG. We call such an activity *compound*, to distinguish it from an *atomic* activity which does not have any possible implementation. To that end, among the activity names in $\mathcal{A}$ we distinguish two disjoint subsets $\mathcal{A} = \mathcal{A}_{atomic} \cup \mathcal{A}_{compound}$, representing atomic and compound activities, respectively. Compound activities can have multiple possible implementations, one of which will be chosen at run-time.

**Definition 2.4   BP specification**    A *BP specification s* is a triple $(S, s_0, \tau)$, where $S$ is a finite set of node-labeled DAGs with labels from $\mathcal{A}$, $s_0 \in S$ is a distinguished DAG consisting of a single node, called the *root*, and $\tau : \mathcal{A}_{compound} \to 2^S$ is the *implementation function*, mapping each compound activity name in $S$ to a *set* of DAGs from $S$. For a compound activity $a$, $\tau(a)$ is referred to as the set of possible implementations of $a$.

We note that a BP specification may be *recursive*, e.g., an implementation of some compound activity in a DAG $s_i$ may be $s_i$ itself.

In effect, BP specifications are similar to Recursive State Machines. An important distinction between the two models is the treatment of executions that encode parallelism, as defined below.

**Example 2.5**    We return to our example of online travel agency. We now interpret Figure 2.3 as a BP specification $s$, and return to some aspects of the process specification, in light of our above definition. The intuitive interpretation of this specification is as follows. The user starts searching for a trip with the *ChooseTravel* activity, at $F1$. *ChooseTravel* has multiple possible implementations, each corresponding to a different choice of search. At runtime, exactly one of them will be chosen. The first possible implementation (denoted by $F2$ in the figure) corresponds to a search of flights, while the second (denoted by $F3$ in the figure) corresponds to a search of combined flight and hotel deals. Within each such implementation, branching models *parallelism*. For instance, in $F2$, the "Advertise" and "Flight" activities occur in parallel (both after the login activity terminates): the "Advertise" activity corresponds to the injection of advertisements to the page, and the "Flight" activity corresponds to a choice of Flight made by the user. After both activities are completed, the user can either confirm, or reset. The latter is possible due to the *recursive* nature of the specification, where a possible implementation of the confirm activity is $F1$, returning to the chooseTravel activity.

### 2.4.1  EXECUTION FLOWS

An EX-flow is modeled as a nested DAG that represents the execution of activities from a BP. Since, in real-life, activities are not instantaneous, we model each occurrence of an activity $a$ by two $a$-labeled nodes, the first standing for the activity *activation* and the second for its *completion* point. These two nodes are connected by an edge. The edges in the DAG represent the ordering among activities activation/completion and the implementation relationships. To emphasize the nested nature of executions, the implementation of each compound activity appears in-between its activation and completion nodes. The structure of an EX-flow must adhere to the structure of the corresponding BP specification, i.e., activities must occur in the same order and implementation relationships must conform to $\tau$.

**Definition 2.6**    Given a BP specification $s = (S, s_0, \tau)$, $e$ is an execution flow (EX-flow) of $s$ if:

- **Base EX-Flow:** $e$ consists only of the activation and completion nodes of the root activity $s_0$ of $s$, connected by a single edge, or;

- **Expansion Step:** $e'$ is an EX-flow of $s$, and $e$ is obtained from $e'$ by attaching, to some start-end pair $(n_1, n_2)$ of an activity $a$ in $e'$ that satisfies condition (*) below, some implementation $e_a$ of $a$, through two new edges, called *implementation edges*, $(n_1, \mathtt{start}(e_a))$ and $(\mathtt{end}(e_a), n_2)$, and annotating the pair with the formula $f_a$ guarding $e_a$.

  (*) We require that this $(n_1, n_2)$ pair does not have any implementation attached to it in $e'$, whereas all its ancestor compound activities in $e'$ do have one.

  In the attached implementation $e_a$, each node is replaced by a corresponding pair of activation and completion nodes, connected by an edge.

  We call $e_a$ a *direct implementation* of $(n_1, n_2)$ and call $e$ an *expansion* of $e'$, denoted $e' \rightarrow e$.

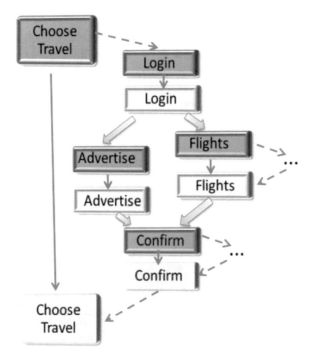

**Figure 2.4:** Execution flow.

We use $e' \to^* e$ to denote that $e$ was obtained from $e'$ by a sequence of expansions. An activity pair in $e$ is *unexpanded* if it is not the source of an implementation edge. We say that an EX-flow is *partial* if it has unexpanded activities, and *full* otherwise, and denote the set of all full flows of a BP specification $s$ by $flows(s)$.

We note that, for recursive BPs, an EX-flow of the BP may be of unbounded size, consisting of an unbounded number of recursive choices. Consequently, the number of (full) EX-flows of such BP is *infinite*.

**Example 2.7**    An execution flow of the travel agency BP is depicted in Figure 2.4. Dashed arrows stand for the implementation relation, and they connect the activation and completion nodes of compound activities to the start and end node (respectively) of the chosen implementation. This execution is obtained for a user that chose to search for hotels only, and this the corresponding implementation is connected to the activation and completion of the ChooseTravel activity. The compound activities in this implementation are the "Hotels" and "Confirm" activity; for each of them a single implementation will be chosen (omitted from the figure).

*Sub-Flows*  We use the phrase "An EX-flow *rooted* at (a compound activity) $A$" to denote the nested DAG obtained by treating $A$ as the root activity and following expansion steps as defined in Definition 2.6. Furthermore, for an EX-flow $e$ and a compound activity node $n$ within $e$, we say that the sub-graph of $e$ appearing in-between the activation and completion nodes of $n$ (i.e., the sub-graph consisting of all nodes and edges such that there exists a directed path from the activation node of $n$ to them, and there exists a directed path from them to the completion node of $n$) is the *sub-flow* of $e$ rooted at $n$.

## 2.4.2  A WEIGHTED MODEL

We next extend the model to allow the assignment of *weights* to possible executions of the Business Process. The weighted model will allow us to distinguish "important" flows from less important ones, as exemplified in the sequel.

Our first step towards a weighted model is to introduce the notion of *guarding formulas*. These are simply predicate calculus formulas used to annotate each possible implementation of every compound activity. We denote the domain of guarding formulas that are in use by $\mathcal{F}$. We next explain how to extend the definitions of business processes and Execution Flows to account for guarding formulas. We will then define weight functions over these formulas, and finally use this definition to define weighted EX-flows.

Recall that the definition of business processes (Definition 2.4) included an implementation function defined as $\tau : \mathcal{A}_{compound} \to 2^S$; to account for guarding formulas, $\tau$ is now defined as $\tau : \mathcal{A}_{compound} \to 2^{S \times \mathcal{F}}$, namely $\tau$ maps each compound activity name to a set of *pairs*, each pair consisting of a guarding formula and a possible implementation graph. Apart from that, the definition of business processes stays intact.

**Example 2.8**  Consider Figure 2.5, and note that the different possible implementation choices for compound activities are annotated with *guarding formulas*, pertaining in this case to possible user choices. For instance, the choice of implementation for the *chooseTravel* activity is dictated by the type of search chosen by the user (e.g., search = "flights only" corresponds to a user choice of searching only for flights, thus leading to F2 where flights are suggested, search = "flights+hotels" to a user choice of searching for flights and hotels thus leading to F3, etc.)

Correspondingly, EX-flows are defined similar to Definition 2.6, but each compound activity in the EX-flow is annotated by the guarding formula corresponding to the implementation chosen for the edge. Note that a given EX-flow (ignoring guarding formulas) may be obtained via different expansion sequences varying in the order of parallel activities expansion.

*Equality and containment of EX-flows*  Given two EX-flows $e$ and $e'$, we use in the sequel the notation $e = e'$ when there exists an isomorphism between $e$ and $e'$ respecting node labels, edge relation and guarding formula names. We say that $e \subseteq e'$ if there exists such isomorphism between $e$ and some EX-flow $e''$ obtained from $e'$ by removing some of its nodes and edges.

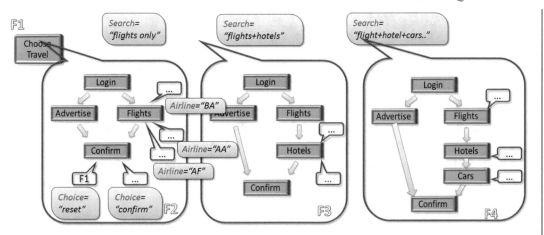

**Figure 2.5:** Weighted model.

We next turn to defining weight functions over BP specifications and execution flows. To that end, we assume an ordered domain $\mathcal{W}$ of weights. We use three functions: (1) $cWeight$ that describes the weight of each implementation choice, given a preceding sub-flow; (2) $aggr$ that aggregates $cWeight$ values; and (3) $fWeight$ that uses $cWeight$ and $aggr$ to compute the weight of an EX-flow.

*The cWeight function*   Given a BP specification $s$, $cWeight$ is a partial function that assigns a weight $w \in \mathcal{W}$ to each pair (partial EX-flow $e$ of $s$, guarding formula $f$ in $s$), such that $f$ guards the compound activity node of $e$ that is next to be expanded. Intuitively, the value $cWeight(e, f)$ is the weight of the implementation guarded by $f$, *given that $e$ is the flow that preceded it.*

**Example 2.9**   Reconsider Figure 2.5; each guarding formula may be associated with a $cWeight$ value, reflecting the *probability* of the choice occurring at run-time; for instance, based e.g., on popularity of choices among previous users, the function may dictate that the probability of a user choice of "flights only," for instance, is 0.5, and those of "flights+hotels" and "flights+hotels+cars" are 0.25, respectively.

**Example 2.10**   Another example for a relevant weight function associates with every possible choice the *monetary cost* that this choice incurs for the user. For instance, the choice of a particular flight will be associated with a weight that is the flight's price, etc.

We distinguish three classes of $cWeight$ functions, called *history-independent*, *bounded-history* and *unbounded-history* functions, reflecting how much of the preceding flow $e$ actually inflicts on the $cWeight$.

*History-independent:* History-independent $cWeight$ functions compute $cWeight(e, f)$ based solely on the choice $f$ and ignore the history $e$ leading to it. Formally, we have the following.

**Definition 2.11**    A $cWeight$ function is history-independent for every guarding formula $f$, $cWeight(e, f) = cWeight(e', f)$ for each two partial EX-flows $e, e'$.

**Example 2.12**    If $cWeight$ corresponds to probability, then history-independence is equivalent to the "Markovian" property [Meyn and Tweedie, 1993]: given the current state (activity), events dictating the following choices are independent of previous choices that were made. For instance, the probability of choosing a particular flight in this case is independent of whether the user chose to search for "flights" or "flights+hotels."

**Example 2.13**    Reconsider the case where $cWeight$ captures monetary cost. If the cost incurred by any every particular choice is independent of other choices (in particular no combined discount deals are suggested), then the weight function is history-independent.

*Bounded-history:* Bounded-history $cWeight$ functions capture the more common scenario where the $cWeight$ value does depend on the history $e$ of the EX-flow, but only in a bounded manner. That is, to determine the $cWeight$ of any implementation choice at an activity node $n$, it suffices to consider only the implementation choices of the last $b$ preceding compound activities, for some bound $b$. By "choice" we refer to the formula guarding the implementation selected for the activity. By "preceding" we refer here to activity nodes $\hat{n}$ that are *ancestors* of $n$ in $e$, i.e., nodes $n'$ such that there exists a directed path from $n'$ to $n$ in $e$ (in contrast to activity nodes that occur in parallel and thus in general may or may not precede $n$).

   More precisely, recall that we assumed that given an EX-flow $e$, the expansion sequence leading to $e$ is well defined. The last choice preceding (the expansion of) a node $n$ in this sequence, denoted $PrevChoice(e, n)$, is the guarding formula of the implementation selected for the last compound activity node $\hat{n}$ in this sequence that preceded $n$ (in the above defined sense). Similarly, $PrevChoice^2(e, n)$ are the last two preceding choices, and more generally $PrevChoice^i(e, n)$ is a *vector* consisting of the $i$ last preceding choices. We are now ready to define bounded-history $cWeight$ functions.

**Definition 2.14**    We say that $cWeight$ is bounded-history, with history bound $b$, if for every activity name $a$, every guarding formula $f$ of $a$, and every two pairs of [EX-flow,next-to-be-expanded-node] $[e, n]$, $[e', n']$ where $\lambda(n) = \lambda(n') = a$ and $PrevChoice^b(e, n) = PrevChoice^b(e', n')$, it holds that $cWeight(e, f) = cWeight(e', f)$.

**Example 2.15**    Bounded-history weight functions allow to capture dependencies between choices. For instance, continuing our running example, if there is a probabilistic dependency between the choice of airline and the choice of search ("Flights Only" or "Flights+Hotels") then this can be captured via a bounded-history weight function, with the bound on relevant history size being 1.

**Example 2.16**    Reconsider weight functions capturing monetary costs. Here bounded-history weight functions can allow to capture notions such as *combined discount deals*, where the price of any particular flight may depend on whether or not a particular hotel reservation was made beforehand.

*Unbounded-history:* Unbounded-history $cWeight$ functions may use an *unbounded* portion of the flow history $e$ to compute the next choice's weight.

**Observation.** Note that, by definition, for non-recursive BPs, $cWeight$ functions are always bounded-history, as even the size of any given EX-flow is bounded. For recursive BPs, on the other hand, the $cWeight$ function may be unbounded-history. However, this is extremely rare in practice.

**Example 2.17**    Note that our example BP is recursive due to the option of "resetting" the search, i.e., going back to the "chooseTravel" activity, an unbounded number of times. If the probability of choosing a particular airline depends on the exact number of times that the user has searched and reset the search, then the corresponding $cWeight$ function designed to capture this probability would be unbounded-history.

**Example 2.18**    As another example, if a BP allows unbounded number of product purchases and the price of a given product depends on the exact number of previously purchased, then the corresponding $cWeight$ function may be unbounded-history.

*The Aggregation function*    The weights along the EX-flow are aggregated using an aggregation function. The function $aggr : \mathcal{W} \times \mathcal{W} \to \mathcal{W}$ receives two weights as inputs; the first is intuitively the aggregated weight computed so far, and the second is the new $cWeight$ to be aggregated with the previous value. For instance, when computing purchase cost $aggr = +$ and $\mathcal{W} = [0, \infty)$; when computing likelihood, $aggr = *$ and $\mathcal{W} = [0, 1]$. We consider here aggregation functions that satisfy the following intuitive constraints.

1. $aggr$ is associative and commutative, namely for each $x, y, z \in \mathcal{W}$, $aggr(aggr(x, y), z) = aggr(x, aggr(y, z))$, and $aggr(x, y) = aggr(y, x)$.

2. $aggr$ is *continuous*, that is for each $x, y, z \in \mathcal{W}$, if $aggr(x, y) < aggr(x, z)$ then there exists $w \in \mathcal{W}$ such that $aggr(x, y) < aggr(x, w) < aggr(x, z)$.

3. $aggr$ has a neutral value, denoted $1_{aggr}$. Namely for each $x \in \mathcal{W}$, $aggr(x, 1_{aggr}) = aggr(1_{aggr}, x) = x$.

4. *aggr* is monotonically increasing or decreasing over $\mathcal{W}$. Namely, either $\forall s, x, y \in \mathcal{W}$  $x \geq y \rightarrow aggr(s, x) \geq aggr(s, y)$ and $aggr(s, x) \geq s$, or the same for $\leq$.

*The fWeight function*   Finally, the $fWeight$ of an EX-flow is obtained by aggregating the $cWeights$ of all choices made during the flow, and is defined recursively: if $e$ is an EX-flow consisting only of the root $s_0$, $fWeight(e) = 1_{aggr}$. Otherwise, , if $e' \to e$ for some EX-flow $e'$ of $s$, then $fWeight(e) = aggr(fWeight(e'), cWeight(e', f))$, where $f$ is the formula guarding the implementation that is added to $e'$ to form $e$.

**Example 2.19**   For cWeight functions capturing choices probabilities, the aggregation function is multiplication: by multiplying the cWeight values of individual choices we obtain the joint distribution of all possible choices (note that the representation of cWeight already encapsulates dependencies, and so multiplication gives the correct result even for the history-dependent case).

**Example 2.20**   For monetary costs, the aggregation function is addition. Here again the representation of cWeight already captures discount deals where such exist.

Observe that both aggregation functions $+$ and $*$, used for cost and likelihood, satisfy the above constraints.

*Weighted BP specifications*   We use the term *weighted BP specification* to refer to a BP specification $s$ along with corresponding weight functions ($cWeight, aggr$ and the derived $fWeight$). When the weight functions are clear from context, we omit them for brevity.

## 2.5   MODELING DATA MANIPULATION

An important aspect in the modeling of business processes is capturing the data manipulation and transformations performed by the process. For instance, in our own Business Process model defined above, the *guarding formulas* that "guard" the possible implementations use data variable. The value of these variables determines the formulas' satisfaction and thus the choice of implementation for each activity. This, in turn, dictates the course of execution. However, the use of data here is limited: guarding formulas may ask for the value of a specific data item, but cannot e.g., issue full-fledged SQL queries on the underlying database to decide on the choice of implementation.

Another example for a limited modeling of data is *scientific workflows* where the interaction between flow and data is given an interesting twist. Scientific workflows are processes that are executed by scientists and composed of modules. Each module performs some scientific task and the modules interact by passing data between them. The workflow specification may be hierarchical, in the sense that a module may be composite and itself implemented as a workflow. The data that are modeled here include the input and output of every module, but not the internal database or the way it is manipulated/queried by the modules. In contrast, this is captured by the models reviewed next.

$$
\begin{aligned}
Ord(user, prod) \quad &+ : - \quad In\,Ord(user, prod) \\
Payed\,Ord(user, prod) \quad &+ : - \quad In\,Payment(user, prod) \\
Unpaid\,Ord(user, prod) \quad &+ : - \quad Ord(user, prod)\ \mathtt{AND} \\
& \qquad\quad \mathtt{NOT}\ Payed\,Ord(user, prod) \\
Out\,Receipt(user, prod) \quad &+ : - \quad Payed\,Ord(user, prod)\ \mathtt{AND} \\
& \qquad\quad In\,Stock(prod)
\end{aligned}
$$

**Figure 2.6:** Relational transducer example.

### 2.5.1    UNDERLYING RELATIONAL DATA

The models that we have mentioned so far mainly focused on the *flow*, i.e., they allow to capture the control flow of a given process, but the data that are manipulated by the process were only modeled to a limited extent. A complementary line of research, in the databases area, resulted in the development of a variety of process models that are centered around data. Such models have appeared even before the term business processes emerged in research, such as the model of Relational Transducers [Abiteboul et al., 1998] (and the follow-up work on ASM transducers [Spielmann, 2003]), that was shown to be very effective in capturing e-commerce applications. In relational transducers, the state of the application is modeled as a relational database and the database state is modified using the repeated activation of queries (in the spirit of active databases [Abiteboul et al., 1995]). The database is used to model not only the internal database state, but also the interaction of the transducer with the external environment: these are modeled via a set of input and output relations. There is thus no clear distinction between the *flow* and the *underlying data* - the database stores it all. A Datalog-like program is used to query and update the state, input and output relations. For instance, the rules in Figure 2.6 can be used to (partially) specify the business logic of an "orders" component of our online travel agency, where payments are made (intuitively, this would follow the "confirmation" stage depicted in our example BP specification). Relation names starting with "In" stand for input relations, those with "Out" for output relations, and the rest are state relations. Here the semantics of the rules is like in inflationary Datalog, that is, a satisfying assignment to the right-hand side leads to an addition of a corresponding tuple for the relation whose name appears on the rule left-hand side.

Note the process flow that is implicit in the above description: the input orders made by the user change the state of the orders, and user payments change the order status from unpaid to paid. *The difficulty is that the underlying flow is not easily observable from the process specification, especially in the common case when the number of state relations is large and inter-dependent.* As a consequence, the process analysts may have difficulty grasping the causality and temporal relationship between data, e.g., which part of the data is influencing other parts, which is updated before the other, etc.

A similar approach is taken in the works on Business Process artifacts [Abiteboul et al., 2011; Fritz et al., 2009; Hull and Su, 2005; Vianu, 2009]. The model focuses on the data received, generated

$$
\begin{array}{rcl}
Artifact\,Class & : & Hotel\,Reservation \\
Hotel & : & string \\
Hotel\,Rating & : & string \\
processed & : & bool \\
Paid\,For & : & bool
\end{array}
$$

**Figure 2.7:** Artifact example.

and manipulated by the process (e.g., purchase orders, sales invoices, etc.). The data structures encapsulating this information are referred to in this context as *artifacts*. An example for such an artifact, for a user reservation of a hotel is given in Figure 2.7. Artifact states are queried and modified by *services*, which are defined by declarative rules, accompanied by pre-and post conditions for their invocation. Again, there is an implicit modeling of flow, since the state of the order (artifact) reflects whether or not it was processed, and whether or not it was paid for, etc. and this information is updated as the flow evolves. But similar to the case of relational transducers, the description of flow is somewhat implicit.

Last, we mention that the modeling of data-centered Web Applications have also received a significant attention in recent years. One notable model in this context is the one of data-driven, interactive Web Applications [Deutsch et al., 2005, 2006] which are essentially implicitly specified *infinite-state machines* in which the state (database) is shared across various applications, each of which may read/write its contents. The interaction of web services, and specifically the data passed between them, were studied also by Bultan et al. [2006].

## 2.5.2   UNDERLYING SEMI-STRUCTURED DATA

Before we conclude, we mention another class of works in this context that considers data which are not relational, but rather semi-structured, and specifically XML. Here again, there are works with an underlying flow model of a finite state machine or context free languages, as well as some probabilistic models. We next review them briefly. The Active XML model [ActiveXml] extends XML with Web Service calls, whose results are embedded in the original document, allowing to make additional calls, etc. In a recent work [Abiteboul et al., 2011] the authors suggest an artifacts model that combines a simple flow model of Finite State Machine, with the data model of Active XML. Also, recent works have studied models for probabilistic XML documents that is based on a generative process modeled by a Recursive State Machine [Benedikt et al., 2010]. In our opinion, these works are important steps towards rich models that combine flow and data; but more work is required to further find the correct balance between the models expressiveness, and the efficiency of query evaluation they allow. Queries on business processes will be discussed in the following chapter.

## 2.6   CONCLUSION AND OPEN ISSUES

In this chapter, we provided an overview of models for business processes. We conclude by listing a few aspects that are absent in the current business processes models, yet we believe are important, and their incorporation is the subject of further research.

- Arguably, the biggest challenge in Business Process modeling is the combination of rich flow model with rich model for underlying database manipulation. As we will see in the next section, high complexity or even undecidability of analysis is difficult to avoid whenever such rich models are considered. We note that Abiteboul et al. [2011] has made a progress in this area by designing an artifact model for Active XML [ActiveXml] with an underlying, explicitly modeled, Finite State Machines. But there is still a long way to go, extending the model expressivity within the boundaries of decidability.

- Cohn and Hull [2009] states that no model is likely to be "the best" for all needs, and consequently that there is a need for the development of a theory (and practical implementations) of *views* on business processes and a practical mapping between them. We concur and believe that this is even more true for rich, combined flow and data model. Recently, there have been a few advancements in this respect. Abiteboul et al. [2011] suggests the notion of a workflow view and use it as a way of comparing expressive power of workflow specification languages. We believe that there are important research challenges in the efficient computation and maintenance of such views.

CHAPTER 3

# Querying Business Processes

As exemplified in Chapter 1, business processes serve as an important information for the processes owners as well as their users. To effectively use this mine of information, we need analysis tools; and to support such tools, what is desired is a formal *query language*.

We next list some of the desired features of such a query language.

- It is desired that such query language will be, like the Business Process specification itself, *declarative*, *intuitive* and *graphical*, allowing the process designer to specify the analysis tasks side by side with the design of the process specification.

- We discussed the importance of models that describe both the process flow and its underlying data. Correspondingly, the query language that is used to analyze the modeled business processes should allow to query *both the process flow and the data*, and the interactions between them.

- The query language should allow to pose queries at different levels of granularity, specified by the analysts. For instance, one may wish to ask coarse-grain queries that consider certain process components as black boxes and allow for high level abstraction, as well as fine-grained queries that "zoom-in" on all or some of the process components, querying there inner-workings.

- The query language should allow to specify "boolean" verification queries, pertaining to the existence of bugs, the enforcement of policies etc, as well as "selection" and "projection" queries that allow to retrieve some parts of the process or its executions, that are relevant for the analysis. For instance, we may not only be interested in the boolean existence of a bug, but if it exists we wish to know in which part of the process it occurred or may occur, under what circumstances, what is may affect, etc.

- Naturally, to make things practical, the query language should allow for efficient query evaluation algorithms and optimizations.

We next review the state-of-the-art in works on querying future and past executions of business processes. We review several lines of work, and then, to provide concrete details on algorithms and complexity results in this context, we focus on the model of [Deutch and Milo, 2008] and show the details of results achieved for the analysis of this model (first in a highlevel in Section 3.2, and then in further details in the following sections). Our discussion towards the end of the chapter (Section 3.7) highlights which of these desired properties were (partially) achieved, and which still remain as challenges.

## 3.1 QUERY FORMALISMS

Given a Business Process specification, analysts are typically interested in testing/querying properties of its possible future executions. The property may be some constraint that is expected to hold in every execution, such as "a user can not place an order without giving her credit card details" or "a user must have a positive balance in her account before placing an order." It may also be the probability that some situation occurs in a random execution, such as "what is the probability that a user chooses to order a particular hotel given that she ordered a particular flight?."

Similar to the case of data analysis, a fundamental effort that should be made, lies in the design of a proper formalism that would be used to express the analysis tasks. In other words, a proper *query language* should be designed.

In what follows, we will review different common formalisms for expressing queries over processes. We then focus on a particular formalism called BPQL, suggested in [Beeri et al., 2007].

### 3.1.1 LINEAR TEMPORAL LOGIC (LTL)

The analysis of possible future executions of a process, also referred to as *static analysis*, was extensively studied for formal flow models (Finite State Machines, Pushdown automata, Context Free Grammars, etc.). The dominant approach for such analysis is to use a *temporal logic* formalism [Emerson, 1990] to query the possible executions of a given process. In (linear) temporal logic, formulas are constructed from predicates and temporal quantifiers such as "before" ($B$), "always" ($A$), "until" ($U$) etc. For instance, a query of the sort "a user must login *before* placing an order" can be expressed by a formula of the form $Login\ B\ Order$, where $Login$ and $Order$ are predicates that can be checked locally on a given flow state.

**Example 3.1** Assume the existence of two predicates, called $Login$ and $Order$ standing, respectively, for the current state corresponding to the login and order pages of the application. Then the analysis question "can a reservation be made without relaying a credit card number?" can be expressed as follows:

- $E(F(Reserve) \bigwedge \neg F(Credit))$.

Similarly, given an additional predicate "search" standing for the user performing a trip search, one can express the analysis question "Must one eventually login if she makes a trip search?" as:

- $A(F(login) \bigvee \neg F(Search))$.

While temporal logic is very useful, it fails to satisfy many of the desiderata in the context of business processes. The main difficulties in using it for analysis of Business Process executions are the following. First, similar to the case of First Order Logic, the design of temporal logic formulas for complicated properties may be cumbersome, and the outcome may be difficult to read. Second, in temporal logic there is no explicit reference to underlying process data, and the properties it allows to capture pertain only to the process flow. Third, it allows only to verify boolean properties, and cannot express any counterpart of selection and projection database queries and, in particular, does not allow to retrieve paths that are of interest.

### 3.1.2   LTL-FO

The shortcoming of explicit constructs for referring to both the flow and data was alleviated by the work of Deutsch et al. [2005], suggesting a query language called LTL-FO (for Linear Temporal Logic-First Order). The idea is that temporal logic is used for querying the execution flow, while first order constructs may be used inside the predicates, for querying not only the execution flow state, but rather the *database* state at the current point of the execution. Here, again, we only provide a sort example and refer the reader to [Deutsch et al., 2005] for definitions, details and evaluation algorithms.

**Example 3.2**    Consider an analysis whose goal is to verify, that in every possible execution, whenever a user places an order for a flight, his balance must be positive. We assume that Order and Balance are database relations. $A$ is the temporal operator "Always" and user, sum, product are used as bound variables in the formula. Then the property stated above is expressed by the following LTL-FO formula:

- $\forall user, product.A(Order(user, product) \Rightarrow \exists sum > 0.balance(user, sum))$.

LTL-FO is an important step in querying business processes. We also mention in this context the work on querying Active XML documents [Abiteboul et al., 2009], introducing tree-LTL, where temporal operators are used over tree patterns. But these languages still lack some of the above desiderata: they do not allow to specify non-boolean queries, do not allow controlled levels of granularity, and they are hard to formulate for non (logic) experts. Before turning to BPQL whose design addresses some of these concerns, we briefly review some main complexity results for the query formalisms described so far.

*Complexity Results*    First, the complexity of evaluation of Linear Temporal Logic (LTL) queries (as well as branching-time logic $CTL^*$ [Emerson, 1990]) on Finite State Machines is known to be linear in the state machine size but exponential in the size of the formula. Alur et al. [2005] show the same complexity results for context free processes, and equivalently for Single Exit RSMs [Etessami and Yannakakis, 2005]. Similarly, for BPQL, the complexity of query evaluation was shown to be polynomial in the process specification size, with the exponent depending on the query size. We mentioned above the query language LTL-FO for querying both flow and data. Deutsch et al. [2004] show that evaluating LTL-FO queries on their process model is *PSPACE-complete* under some restrictive assumptions on the input process, and is undecidable in general (although a practical implementation based on strong heuristics was developed by Deutsch et al. [2005]). It is observable that the blowup in the complexity of query evaluation is difficult to avoid when querying flow and data together. Finding a framework that will satisfy all of the above-listed desiderata, and will in particular allow for efficient query evaluation, is an important research challenge.

### 3.1.3    BPQL

Some of the desiderata that are not achieved by the different variants of temporal logic (with or without constructs for querying data) are satisfied by BPQL (Business Process Querying Language) [Beeri et al., 2007], allowing for the posing of queries on our Business Process model. BPQL is based on abstraction of the Business Process Execution Language (BPEL) [bpel] formalism, along with a graphical user interface that allows for simple formulation of queries on BPEL specifications. At the core of the BPQL language are Business Process *patterns* that allow users to describe the pattern of activities/data flow that are of interest. Business Process patterns are similar to the tree and graph-patterns offered by query languages for XML and graph-shaped data, but include two novel features designed to address the above desiderata. First, BPQL supports navigation along two axis: (1) the standard path-based axis, that allows to navigate through, and query, paths in process graphs; and (2) a novel zoom-in axis, that allows to navigate (transitively) inside process components and query them at any depth of nesting. Second, paths are considered first class objects in BPQL and can be retrieved, and represented compactly. We next provide the formal definitions for BPQL.

Queries are defined using *execution patterns* (abbr. EX-patterns), which generalize execution flows (EX-flows) in a similar way to the way tree patterns generalize XML trees. EX-patterns are EX-flows where activity names are either specified, or left open using a special ANY symbol. Edges in a pattern are either regular, interpreted over edges, or transitive, interpreted over paths. Similarly, activity pairs may be regular or transitive, for searching only in their direct implementation or for searching in any nesting depth, respectively.

**Definition 3.3    Execution Patterns**    An *execution pattern*, abbr. EX-pattern, is a pair $p = (\hat{e}, T)$ where $\hat{e}$ is an EX-flow whose nodes are labeled by labels from $\mathcal{A} \cup \{any\}$, and $T$ is a distinguished set of activity pairs and edges in $\hat{e}$, called *transitive* activities and edges, resp.

**Example 3.4**    An example EX-pattern is depicted in Figure 3.1 (ignore for now the shaded rectangle). The pattern seeks for all possible EX-flows where the user logs in, then makes some choice of airline, and then confirms his choice. The query looks, visually, very similar to an EX-flow: it has compound activities (such as `Flight`) to which an implementation is attached through implementation edges, and atomic activities (such as `Login`). Two distinctions are apparent in the figure: first, the `Flight` activity node is *doubly bounded*, signaling that it is *transitive*. Intuitively, this means that

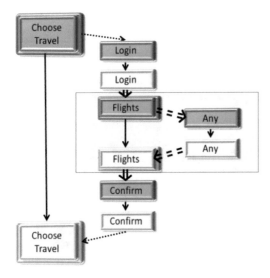

Figure 3.1:  EX-pattern.

we wish to seek for the occurrence of an airline choice in its *indirect* implementation (i.e., in the implementation of Flight, or in an implementation of one of the compound nodes appearing in its implementation, etc.). Another difference is the existence of *transitive edges*, denoted as doubly arrowed edges (see for instance the edge connecting Flight and Confirm). This means that it may match any path of activity nodes appearing, in the EX-flow of interest, in-between the Flight and the Confirm nodes.

Observe that apart from the transitive nodes and edges, EX-patterns and EX-flows look similar, making the formulation of queries rather intuitive.

To evaluate a query, the EX-pattern is matched against a given EX-flow. A match is represented by an *embedding*.

**Definition 3.5  Embedding**    Let $p = (\hat{e}, T)$ be an EX-pattern and let $e$ be an EX-flow. An embedding of $p$ into $e$ is a homomorphism $\psi$ from the nodes and edges in $p$ to nodes, edges and paths in $e$ such that:

1. **[nodes]** Activity pairs in $p$ are mapped to activity pairs in $e$. Node labels are preserved; however, a node labeled by *any* can be mapped to nodes with any activity name. The root activity pair of $p$ must be mapped to the root activity pair of $e$.

2. **[edges]** Each (transitive) edge from node $m$ to node $n$ in $p$ is mapped to an edge (path) from $\psi(m)$ to $\psi(n)$ in $e$. If the edge $[m, n]$ belongs to a direct implementation of a *transitive* activity,

the edge (edges on the path) from $\psi(m)$ to $\psi(n)$ can be of any type (flow, or implementation) and otherwise must have the same type as $[m, n]$.

We say that an EX-flow $e$ *qualifies* with respect to an EX-pattern $p$ if there exists an embedding of $p$ in $e$.

## BPQL QUERY TYPES

Using the notion of execution patterns, we may further define queries over *BP specifications*. Multiple semantics may be of interest here, depending on the analysis goal in hand. In particular, we will be interested in: (1) *selection queries*, that select all matches of qualifying EX-flows of a given specification with respect to the given EX-pattern; (2) *projection queries*, where only parts (sub-flows) of the matched EX-flows are of interest; and (3) *boolean queries* that ask for the existence of such qualifying EX-flows (or for the probability of obtaining one in a random execution, for weighted BPs where weights correspond to probabilities).

Note that since recursive BP specifications may in general define infinitely many EX-flows, there may also be infinitely many results for both selection and projection queries when evaluated with respect to a given BP. Even in the non-recursive case, the number of results may be extensively large (exponential in the size of the BP specification). Thus, rather than enumerating *all* results, we will focus on computing the *top-k* ones, based on a ranking function that is itself based on the weight function given as input (to be defined precisely in the sequel). Of course, there is no sense in defining top-k results for boolean queries; instead, for boolean queries we will focus on a particular case of weighted BPs, namely the case where the weights reflect *probabilities*. As shall be observed, this case fits into the large picture, as boolean queries serve as important auxiliary tools for the evaluation of top-k projection queries under the *sum* semantics on probabilistic BPs.

We next define the different semantics, and then, in the following sections, turn to design algorithms for query evaluation with respect to these semantics.

*Selection queries*   A selection query is represented by an EX-pattern, and the semantics is defined as follows.

**Definition 3.6   Selection queries semantics**   Given a selection query captured by an execution pattern $p$ and a BP specification $s$, we define the result of evaluating $p$ over $s$, denoted by $p(s)$, as the set of all EX-flows of $s$ that qualify according to $p$.

**Example 3.7**   Re-consider the BP specification $s$ depicted in Figure 2.5, and the EX-pattern $p$ in Figure 3.1 (ignoring the shaded rectangle). $p$ can be embedded in any execution flow where the user logs-in, performs any sequence of activities (to match the transitive edge between the Login and Flights activities, then makes any choice of flights (corresponding to the implementation of the Flights activity, or implementation of activities occurring in such implementation, and so forth, at any nesting depth), then any sequence of choices (e.g., for hotels and cars), and then confirm.

In contrast, note that if the `ChooseTravel` activity and its implementation edges were *transitive*, then the semantics entails also matches to EX-flows where the user makes repeated choices and cancellations, followed eventually by the choice of some flight (since implementations of transitive nodes can match activities in any implementation nesting level).

*Observation*   If the BP specification $s$ is recursive, the set $p(s)$ may be of infinite cardinality.

*Boolean queries*   Under the boolean semantics, we ask for the *existence* of an EX-flow of the given BP specification that qualifies with respect to the given EX-pattern.

**Definition 3.8   Boolean query semantics**   Given a boolean query captured by an execution pattern $p$ and a BP specification $s$, we define the result of evaluating $p$ as a boolean query over $s$, denoted by $p^b(s)$, to be *true* if there exists a qualifying EX-flow of $s$ with respect to $p$.

**Example 3.9**   Consider again the EX-pattern $p$ in Figure 3.1; when treated as a boolean query evaluated with respect to the BP specification $s$ of our running example, we only ask for the existence of an EX-flow of $s$ that qualifies with respect to $p$. Since there exist such flows, the evaluation result is *true*.

*Projection queries*   For *projection* queries, the EX-pattern $p$ is accompanied by a specification of a sub-pattern called the *projected part*. Similar to selection queries, the query focuses attention on qualifying EX-flows, but then further limits the result to the sub-flows that were matched against the projected part of the pattern.

**Definition 3.10   Projection queries**

A projection query $q = (p, P)$ consists of an execution pattern $p$ accompanied by a sub-graph $P$ of the pattern, itself forming an execution pattern, called the *projected* part of the pattern.

The result of a projection query is defined as follows.

- Given an embedding $h$ of $p$ in an EX-flow $e$, we use $h{\downarrow}_P$ to denote the graph consisting of the nodes and edges of $e$ to which $h$ maps the nodes and edges of the projected part $P$. We say that two embeddings $h, h'$ of $p$ in two (possibly isomorphic) EX-flows $e, e'$ are *equivalent* if $h{\downarrow}_P$ is isomorphic to $h'{\downarrow}_P$. We further denote $\Psi$ as a set consisting of a single representative from each such equivalence class of embeddings.

- For an EX-flow $e$ and an embedding $h$ of $p$ in $e$, the result of $q$ on $e$, w.r.t. $h$, is denoted $q_{\downarrow}(e, h)$ and contains all nodes and edges of $P$, with $Any$-labels of nodes in $P$ replaced by activity names of the nodes in $e$ they are mapped to by $h$, and transitive edges in $P$ replaced by the paths they are mapped to by $h$. For each activity pair appearing in the result, the edge connecting its activation and completion nodes is also included.

- For an EX-flow $e$, the result of $q$ on $e$, denoted $q_{\downarrow}(e)$, consists of the results of all possible embeddings of $q$ into $e$, i.e., $q_{\downarrow}(e) = \bigcup_{h \in \Psi} q_{\downarrow}(e, h)$.

- Finally, for a BP $s$, the result of $q$ on $s$, denoted $q_{\downarrow}(s)$ is the set of all possible results of $q$ when applied on the EX-flows of $s$. Namely, $q_{\downarrow}(s) = \bigcup_{e \in flows(s)} q_{\downarrow}(e)$.

**Example 3.11**   Re-consider the EX-pattern $p$ in Figure 3.1, and note now the part of the pattern in the shaded rectangle. This is the projected part $P$. When evaluated with respect to our running example BP specification $s$, the result consists of projecting out the parts of the embeddings in the qualifying flows, that correspond to $P$, namely, the part of these flows that corresponds to the choice of implementation to the Flights activity, intuitively corresponding to the choice of airline.

*Top-k queries*   For the above definitions we have considered all possible EX-flows of the BP specification that match the EX-pattern as results. However, recall our notion of weighted BP specifications that allows to distinguish between different executions based on their importance. Leveraging this notion for the semantics of queries, we will in fact consider top-k variations for each of the query types discussed above. The output of these queries is a ranked list of results, ordered by rate. We next define top-k selection and projection queries. As we will observe, boolean queries will serve as tools for the evaluation of top-k projection queries.

**Definition 3.12  Top-k selection queries**   The top-k results of a selection query $p$ with respect to a weighted BP specification $s$, denoted top-k$(p, s)$ are the $k$ EX-flows having the highest $fWeight$ out of the EX-flows in $p(s)$.

**Example 3.13**   Consider the cWeight function (reflecting probabilities) in Table 3.2, dictating weights of guarding formulas occurring in the BP specification in Figure 2.5. Note that out of all EX-flows in $p(s)$, the highest $fWeight$ is obtained for the one containing "Flight Only" choice and then the choice of $BA$ airline (followed by EX-flows containing the "Flight Only" choice with any of the two airlines; the $fWeight$ value of these EX-flows are tied), thus it is the top-1 result.

The definition of top-k projection queries is a bit more subtle. Note that an EX-flow $e' \in q_{\downarrow}(s)$ may originate from several EX-flows of $s$, namely there may be several $e \in flows(s)$ s.t. $e' \in q_{\downarrow}(e)$.

| $searchType$ | P($searchType$) | $airline$ | P($airline$) |
|---|---|---|---|
| "flights only" | 0.5 | "BA" | 0.7 |
| "flights+hotels" | 0.25 | "AF" | 0.2 |
| "flights+hotels+cars" | 0.25 | "AL" | 0.1 |
| $hotel$ | P($hotel$) | $choice$ | P($choice$) |
| "Marriott" | 0.6 | "reset" | 0.6 |
| "HolidayInn" | 0.3 | "confirm" | 0.2 |
| "CrownePlaza" | 0.1 | "cancel" | 0.2 |

**Figure 3.2:** Cweight function reflecting choices probabilities.

For instance, continuing our running example, any two EX-flows that share the same choice of airline results in the same EX-flow obtained for the example query.

Before defining the top-k projection results, we should first decide on how to aggregate the weights of these individual EX-flows, to form the score of projection result.

We will consider two possible aggregation functions (and consequently, semantics of queries), *max* and *sum*. Under *max* semantics, the *score* of $e'$ is defined as $score(e') = max\{fWeight(e) \mid e \in flows(s) \land e' \in q_{\downarrow}(e)\}$. Under *sum* semantics, $score(e') = \sum_{e \in flows(s) \land e' \in q_{\downarrow}(e)} fWeight(e)$.

**Definition 3.14  Top-k projection queries**  The top-k results of a projection query $q$ over a BP specification $s$, with respect to *max* (*sum*) semantics, denoted top-$k_{max}(q_{\downarrow}, s)$ (top-$k_{sum}(q_{\downarrow}, s)$), is a set of EX-flows in $q_{\downarrow}(s)$ having highest score values according to *max* (*sum*) semantics, respectively. When the semantics used is clear from context, we omit it from the notation and simply write top-k($q_{\downarrow}, s$).

**Example 3.15**  We next illustrate the difference between *max* and *sum* semantics. Consider a case where a particular combined flight+hotel deal is very popular, but where packages consisting of flight and hotel reservations are *overall* more common. Now, consider the query above that wishes to identify how a package that includes a flight reservation is typically booked. With *sum* semantics, the flight+hotel option is ranked highest, as it appears in most EX-flows. But with *max* semantics, flight+car would be ranked highest, as there exists one very popular EX-flow where it appears.

## 3.2    OVERVIEW OF COMPLEXITY RESULTS

In the following sections we study algorithms for evaluating BPQL on weighted BPs, for the types of queries defined above. Before reviewing the algorithms themselves, we briefly overview the complexity model that is used here, and the complexity of our query evaluation algorithms in the different contexts.

| Input | Query | Select | Proj$_{max}$ | **Bool** | **Proj$_{sum}$** |
|---|---|---|---|---|---|
| Recursive | General | PTIME | PTIME | **EXPTIME (approx.)** | **EXPTIME** |
| | Restricted | PTIME | PTIME | **EXPTIME (approx.)** | **EXPTIME** |
| Non-Recursive | General | PTIME | PTIME | **EXP/PTIME (exact)** | **EXPTIME** |
| | Restricted | PTIME | PTIME | **EXP/PTIME (exact)** | **EXP/PTIME** |

**Figure 3.3:** Data complexity of query evaluation for the different query types.

We will focus on results for *top-k* query evaluation, which, as explained above, are of the most practical interest.

*Complexity Model*   When analyzing the complexity of query evaluation, one may consider *data complexity* and *combined complexity* [Vardi, 1982]. Data complexity is the complexity of evaluating a query as a function of the *database* size, while *combined complexity* is a function of both the database and the query sizes. In our case, the "data" is typically the given BP specification while the query is the EX-pattern, and the notions of data complexity and combined complexity are adapted correspondingly.

We note that there is an interesting difficulty in the context of projection queries with sum semantics, that lies in the size of numbers that are manipulated. In particular, we show below that the probabilities that should be outputted for query answers may be so small that their exact representation (where possible) requires exponentially many bits with respect to the input representation size. When analyzing the complexity of algorithms, one may either take into account the representation and manipulation of these numbers (as in the Turing-model complexity analysis), or may alternatively assume that arithmetic operations require O(1) time, regardless of the numbers size (this is referred to as the unit-cost RAM model with exact rational arithmetic [Blum et al., 1998]). Where relevant, we analyze our algorithms with respect to both computational models.

*Complexity results*   Table 3.3 summarizes our data complexity results for top-k selection queries ("Select"), top-k projection queries with *sum* or *max* semantics ("Proj$_{max}$" or "Proj$_{sum}$," respectively), or boolean queries ("Bool") over (recursive or non-recursive) weighted BPs, with history-independent weight function[1]. When the weight function is history-bounded, the complexity results go through, but with an added exponential dependency on the history bound. In the notations used in the table, EXP/PTIME means PTIME under unit-cost arithmetic model (i.e., when we assume that arithmetic operations can be performed in O(1) regardless of the size of bit representation of the input), and EXPTIME under Turing Computational model (i.e., when the size of numeric representation is taken into account in the complexity analysis). "Approx" means that the computed result is approximated up to any given $\epsilon$. The exact restrictions on the query language that are mentioned in the table will be defined in the sequel.

---

[1]The results for boolean queries and projection queries with *sum* semantics are known to hold only for the particular case where the weight function reflects probabilities; it may be possible to extend them to general weight functions, but this is not yet known.

# 3.3   EVALUATION OF SELECTION QUERIES

We start our description of query evaluation algorithms with the case of selection queries, and here we begin by considering first the simpler case where *every* EX-flow qualifies according to the pattern. In other words, we are looking for the top-k EX-flows of the BP specification, without restricting the attention to those qualifying to a particular pattern. We will observe that a solution to this problem will serve as an important building block for query evaluation.

Given a weighted BP specification $s$ and a number $k$, we use top-k(s) to denote the set of $k$ EX-flows in $flows(s)^2$. We refer to the problem of identifying top-k(s) (given the above input) as TOP-K-FLOWS. We start by solving TOP-K-FLOWS for BP specifications accompanied by a history-independent $cWeight$ function; bounded-history and unbounded-history functions are considered in Section 3.3.3.

We give next an efficient algorithm for TOP-K-FLOWS. As the algorithm is intricate, we present it gradually: we start with a simple variant, explain its operation, then analyze its correctness and show cases where it fails. Consequently, we refine it to obtain the correct algorithm.

## 3.3.1   FIRST (UNSUCCESSFUL) ATTEMPT

The FindFlows procedure given in Algorithm 1 attempts to compute the top-k EX-flows of a given BP. (Ignore for now the boxed lines). Its input a BP specification $s$, a weight function over its EX-flows, represented by $cWeight$ and $aggr$, and the number $k$ of requested results. Its output is an ordered queue $Out$ of results. The algorithm uses a function AllExps that, given a partial EX-flow $e$ returns all EX-flows $e'$ s.t. $e \rightarrow e'$, along with their corresponding guarding formulas $F'$.

The algorithm operates in the spirit of the $A^*$ [Dechter and Pearl, 1985] search algorithm: it considers, in a greedy manner, the possible EX-flows of $s$, and computes the $fWeight$ of each. The computation may be viewed as a gradual generation of a *search tree*, whose nodes correspond to possible (partial or full) EX-flows. The search tree root is an EX-flow consisting of only the BP root; at each step, we choose a leaf $e$ in the search tree, and consider all of its possible next expansions. Each such expansion $e'$ becomes a child of $e$, and the computation continues. We next explain how this search tree is generated.

The algorithm maintains a priority queue $Frontier$ of (partial) EX-flows (ordered by $fWeight$) that need to be considered. Initially, it contains a single partial EX-flow, containing only the BP root (line 2). At each step, we pop the highest weighted flow $e$ from $Frontier$ (line 4). If $e$ is a full flow, we insert it to the output queue $Out$ (line 6). This is justified in Theorem 3.16 below. Otherwise, we invoke $HandleExps$ over $e$. $HandleExps$, depicted in Algorithm 2, considers all possible direct expansions $e'$ of $e$, obtained by choosing some implementation, guarded by $F'$, at the next-to-be-expanded node (lines 1-2). It computes the weight of each such EX-flow and inserts it to (the global variable) $Frontier$ (lines 3-4).

---

[2] Certain EX-flows may have equal weights, which implies that there may be several valid solutions to the problem, in which case we pick one arbitrarily.

**Input**: $s; cWeight; aggr; k$
**Output**: $Out$
1 Initialize $Frontier$ and $Out$ ;
2 Push $(s_0, 1_{aggr})$ in $Frontier$ ;
3 **while** $|Frontier| > 0 \land |Out| < K$ **do**
4    $(e, w_e) \leftarrow pop(Frontier)$ ;
5    **if** $e$ *is a full EX-flow* **then**
6     insert $(e, w_e)$ into $Out$        $\boxed{HandleFullFlow(e, w_e)}$ ;
7    **else**
8     $HandleExps(e)$        $\boxed{refinedHandleExps(e)}$ ;
9 **end**
10 **return** Out;

**Algorithm 1:** FindFlows $\boxed{\text{refinedFindFlows}}$

*Properties of the Basic Algorithm*   We next analyze Algorithm 1. On the positive side, we show that the algorithm inserts EX-flows to $Out$ in a correct order. As a consequence, the algorithm is *valid*, i.e., if it terminates, $Out$ contains the top-k EX-flows.

**Theorem 3.16**   At any point of the execution of Algorithm FindFlows, there exist no $e, e' \in flows(s)$ such that $e \in Out$, $e' \in flows(s) - Out$, and $fWeight(e) < fWeight(e')$.

**Proof.** The proof works by contradiction. Let us assume the existence of such $e, e'$. We say that $e''$ is an ancestor of $e'$ if $e'' \rightarrow^* e'$, and denote by $e''$ the lowest ancestor of $e'$ that was already in $Frontier$ at the time of moving $e$ to $Out$ (there exists such flow, perhaps consisting only of the root). $fWeight(e) \geq fWeight(e'')$, otherwise $e$ would have not been moved to $Out$. But $fWeight(e'') \geq fWeight(e')$ by monotonicity, thus $fWeight(e) \geq fWeight(e')$.   □

On the negative side, the algorithm has two significant drawbacks. First, when the BP contains recursion, the algorithm may repeatedly choose recursive expansions and *fail to halt*. Second, note that the algorithm explicitly generates EX-flows. As the size of even a single EX-flow may be exponential in the BP size, this may be costly (even for non-recursive BP specifications).

We next show an example for a case where the algorithm does not terminate.

**Example 3.17**   Consider, for instance, the following recursive BP specification, with $cWeight$ values in the range [0, 1], and $aggr = *$. Its root activity $A$ has two possible implementations: the first, guarded by a formula with $cWeight$ of 0, consists of a single atomic activity $a$. The second, guarded by a formula with $cWeight$ of 0.5, consists of a recursive invocation of $A$. The algorithm will

---

**Input**: e
1  $Expansions \leftarrow AllExps(e)$ ;
2  **foreach** $(e', F') \in Expansions$ **do**
3     |  $r_{e'} \leftarrow aggr(r_e, cWeight(e, F'))$ ;
4     |  insert $(e', r_{e'})$ into $Frontier$;
5  **end**

---

**Algorithm 2:** HandleExps

keep considering recursive expansions of $A$, each time obtaining EX-flows with decreasing weight, but nevertheless higher than 0, and will never terminate.

We next present a refined version of the algorithm that ensures both termination and efficiency, while maintaining a compact representation of the EX-flows.

### 3.3.2   THE REFINED ALGORITHM

The refined version of the algorithm is based on two observations. Before presenting them, recall that we have defined above the $fWeight$ function only for EX-flows that originate from the BP root activity. However, the definition naturally extends to sub-flows originating from an arbitrary compound activity node $n$ in the EX-flow (treating it as a root). Namely, all $cWeight$ values are defined as before, with $fWeight$ aggregating only $cWeight$ values within the sub-flow rooted at $n$.

**Observation 1.** We first observe that distinct activity nodes $n, n'$ (appearing in the same or in different EX-flows) sharing the same activity name, are in fact *equivalent*, in the sense that every sub-flow that may originate from $n$ may also originate from $n'$, having exactly the same $fWeight$[3]. An algorithm may exploit this to compute $fWeight$ values just once for each activity name.

**Observation 2.** Second, observe that the monotonicity of $fWeight$ facilitates incremental-style computation, i.e., the $j$'th ranked sub-flow rooted at an activity node $n$ can use only better ranked sub-flows rooted at nodes sharing the same activity name as $n$. More formally (recall that $\lambda(n)$ stands for the activity name labeling a node $n$),

**Lemma 3.18**

1. *There exists a best-ranked (top $-1$) EX-flow originating at $n$ that contains no occurrence of any other node $n'$ such that $\lambda(n') = \lambda(n)$.*

2. *For $j > 1$, there exists a $j$-th ranked flow originating at $n$ such that for any occurrence of a node $n'$ for which $\lambda(n') = \lambda(n)$ in it, the sub-flow rooted at $n'$ is one of the top $(j - 1)$ such sub-flows.*

---

[3]Recall that we are currently assuming that $cWeight$ is history independent, and relax this assumption in Section 3.3.3.

*Proof.* Let $n$ be a compound activity node, and let $a$ be the compound activity name labeling $n$.

1. Assume that there exists a best weighted EX-flow $e$ rooted at $n$ violating condition (1) above, i.e., $e$ contains another node $n'$ labeled by $a$. Denote the sub-flow rooted at $n'$ as $e'$. Note (see observation 1 above) that every EX-flow rooted at $n'$ may also be treated as an EX-flow rooted at $n$, and its $fWeight$ remains intact.

   Further note that $e' \subseteq e$, and thus (from the monotonicity of fWeight) it follows that $fWeight(e') \geq fWeight(e)$, and further $e'$ contains one less occurrences of nodes labeled by $a$. If $e'$ still contains a node labeled by $a$, we may repeat the process to eliminate it, and so forth. If the original EX-flow $e$ contains $m$ nodes labeled by $a$ (in addition to the root $n$), this process terminates after $m$ steps, with an EX-flow rooted at $n$ that contains no nodes labeled by $a$ (apart for $n$ itself). The fWeight of the obtained EX-flow is greater or equal to the fWeight of $e$.

2. Let $e$ be a $(j + 1)$'th EX-flow rooted at $n$ that violates the lemma, i.e., it contains another node $n'$ labeled by $a$ such that the sub-flow rooted at $n'$ is not one of the top-j such sub-flows. Then we may replace the sub-flow rooted at $n'$ by one of the top-$j$ sub-flows. By monotonicity of the weight function, the obtained flow $e'$ bears at least the same $fWeight$ as $e$; by the inductive assumption there exists a set of top-j EX-flows such that $e'$ may not be obtained in the above manner, and thus can serve as the (j+1)-ranked flow in this set. We obtain a set of top-(j+1) flows satisfying the lemma constraint.

□

Let us illustrate the implications of this Lemma.

**Example 3.19**   Re-consider Example 3.17, and recall that while trying to retrieve the top-1 EX-flow rooted at $A$, FindFlows has encountered a recursive invocation of $A$, and has examined possible EX-flows of the latter, thus resulting in an infinite loop. Following Lemma 3.18, this is redundant: to compute the top-1 EX-flow one may avoid considering flows that contain a recursive call to $A$. The top-2 flow may contain a recursive invocation of $A$, but the only sub-flow that needs to be considered as potential expansion for this occurrence of $A$ is the (already computed) top-1 flow, and so on.

*Algorithm*   Following observation 1, we define an EX-flows table, $FTable$, which (compactly) maintains the top-k (sub)flows rooted at each compound activity name appearing in the BP specification. It has rows corresponding to compound activity names, and columns ranging from 1 to $k$. Each entry contains a pointer to the corresponding sub-flow.

The refined TOP-K algorithm, depicted in Algorithm 3, operates in two steps: first it calls a refined version of FindFlows which computes a compact representation of the top-k EX-flows, then it calls `EnumerateFlows` (depicted below) to explicitly enumerate the EX-flows from this compact representation.

---

**Input**: $s; cWeight; aggr; k$
**Output**: top-k
1  Initialize $FTable$ ;
2  $tmp \leftarrow refinedFindFlows(s, cWeight, aggr, k)$ ;
3  top-k $\leftarrow EnumerateFlows(tmp)$ ;
4  return top-k ;

---

**Algorithm 3:** TOP-K

---

**Input**: e
1  $v \leftarrow getNext(e)$ ;
2  $TableRow = FTable.findEntry(v)$ ;
3  **if** $TableRow = NULL$ **then**
4      Create a new frow for $v$ in $FTable$ ;
5      $HandleExps(e)$ ;
6  **end**
7  **else**
8      $UnhandledExp \leftarrow \{e'_v \in TableRow \mid e'_v$ was not chosen for v when preceded by $e\}$ ;
9      **if** $UnhandledExp = NULL$ **then**
10          insert $((e, w_e), v)$ into $OnHold$ ;
11      **end**
12      **else**
13          $e''_v \leftarrow top(UnhandledExp)$ ;
14          $e' \leftarrow$ expand e by *pointing* v to $e''_v$;
15          $w_{e'} \leftarrow aggr(w_e, fWeight(e''_v))$ ;
16          insert $(e', w_{e'})$ into $Frontier$;
17      **end**
18  **end**

---

**Algorithm 4:** refinedHandleExps

First, we explain the `refinedFindFlows` procedure. The changes, relative to what we have previously seen in Algorithm 1, are depicted in the boxed lines (of this algorithm): The treatment of full EX-flows (in line 6) is replaced by a more refined treatment, performed by the `HandleFullFlow` procedure (depicted in Algorithm 5). The treatment of partial EX-flows is also refined: the generation of candidate expansions (line 8), previously performed by `HandleExps` is now performed by the refined variant `refinedHandleExps` (depicted in Algorithm 4). These two new procedures will be in charge, among others, of the construction of $FTable$. The variable $Out$ (that previously explicitly enumerated the top-k EX-flows) now contains a compact representation of the flows, based on this $FTable$. We next explain these two procedures.

*refinedHandleExps*   The refined treatment of candidate expansions is detailed in Algorithm 4. For the next-to-be-expanded node $v$ in $e$ (line 1), we look up its entry in $FTable$ (line 2). If no entry is found, it means that we haven't encountered yet an equivalent node (i.e., a node sharing the same compound activity name) during the computation. We thus create a new row in $FTable$ for this activity name (line 4). Entries in this row will be filled later, when corresponding full flows are found. Then, we process $v$'s expansions as before (line 5) using Algorithm 2.

Otherwise, if the appropriate row already exists in the table, we consider the partial EX-flows that appear in this row but were not yet considered for expanding $e$ (line 8). If no such EX-flow exists, (although the table entry itself does exist), it means that $e$ was previously reached when expanding some other node $v'$ (which appears in $e$ as well). Following observation 2, we may compute the next best EX-flow without computing further expansions of $e$. Thus, we put $e$ on hold (line 10). It will be released only later, upon finding a full flow originating in $v'$ (see below). Else (i.e., an unused EX-flow does exist), we take the highest ranked such EX-flow and simply "hang" it on $v$, that is, we make $v$ point to this flow (lines 13-14). Finally, we now compute the weight of the obtained EX-flow (line 15) and insert it into $Frontier$, for further expansions (line 16).

---

**Input**: $e, w_e$

1 insert $(e, w_e)$ into $Out$ ;

2 **foreach** *node* $n \in e$ **do**

3 $\quad$ $e_n^{rooted} \leftarrow$ the sub-flow of $e$ rooted at $n$;

4 $\quad$ $w_n^{rooted} \leftarrow fWeight(f_n^{rooted})$ ;

5 $\quad$ **if** *not* $(e_n^{rooted} \in FTable)$ **then**

6 $\quad\quad$ $FTable.update(n, e_n^{rooted})$ ;

7 $\quad$ **end**

8 $\quad$ **foreach** $(e', n) \in OnHold$ **do**

9 $\quad\quad$ insert $e'$ into $Frontier$ ;

10 $\quad$ **end**

11 **end**

**Algorithm 5:** HandleFullFlow

---

*HandleFullFlow*   The refined treatment of full EX-flows is detailed in Algorithm 5. As before, full EX-flows are inserted into $Out$ (line 1). Additionally, for every node appearing in the EX-flow, `HandleFullFlow` fills in the corresponding entry in $FTable$. The sub-flow rooted at the node is inserted into the table, if it does not appear there already (lines 3-7). Last, all EX-flows that are on hold due to a node participating in the full EX-flow, are returned to Frontier (lines 8-9).

To conclude, let us explain how `EnumerateFlows` extracts the flows from their compact representation in *Out*.

*EnumerateFlows*    The EX-flows in *Out* contain activity nodes that point to entries in the *FTable*, describing the sub-flow rooted at the nodes. The nodes in each such description also possibly point to other table entries describing the structure of the sub flow rooted at them and so on. *Enumerateflows* thus simply follows these pointers to materialize the full EX-flow. This pointer chasing is guaranteed to terminate since, following observation 2, pointers in *FTable* induce no loops.

**Example 3.20**    Consider again the BP specification from Example 3.17 and assume that we want to compute its top-2 flows. Starting with the root activity $A$, `refinedHandleExps` looks for its equivalence class in *FTable*. Since the table is empty, a new equivalence class containing only $A$ is defined, and a row is generated for it in *FTable*. Then, the possible expansions of $A$ are examined (Line 5 of `refinedHandleExps`), and two possible expansions are added to the Frontier: one full EX-flow (denote by $f1$), corresponding to the implementation choice leading to the atomic activity $a$, and one partial flow (denote by $f2$), containing a recursive invocation of $A$. Next, $f2$, having the better $cWeight$, is popped out of *Frontier*. The next activity to be expanded in $f2$ is $A$, but as it appears in the table, this expansion is removed from *Frontier* and stays on hold (Line 10). Then $f1$ is the only EX-flow in *Frontier* and is popped, then inserted to *Out* by `HandleFullFlow` (Indeed, $f1$ is the top-1 flow). Now, the entry in *FTable* for the top-1 flow rooted at $A$ is updated to be $fWeight(f1)$, and $f2$ is "released" from *OnHold* and returned to *Frontier* (lines 8-9 of `HandleFullFlow`), for computation of the 2nd-best EX-flow.

*Correctness*    We next show that Algorithm `TOP-K` is correct.

**Theorem 3.21**    Algorithm `TOP-K` halts and returns the top-k weighted EX-flows of the input BP $s$.

*Proof.* Following the validity of our basic $A^*$-like Algorithm, to prove the theorem it remains to show that (1) the revised version terminates and (2) the order in which partial EX-flows are inserted to *Out*, in the revised algorithm, does not harm the validity. We next prove both claims.

1. Consider the computation of the top-1 flow rooted at a compound activity name $a$. Assume that during this computation, we get to a flow $e$ whose next node to be expanded $v$ is also labeled by $a$. At this point, the *FTable* row corresponding to $a$ is empty. Consequently, at lines 9-11 of `refinedHandleExps`, $e$ will be put on hold and is not further expanded throughout the top-1 computation. This will happen for each such $e$. Similarly, if during the computation of the top-1 flow rooted at a compound activity name $a$, we start computing the

top-1 flow rooted at $b$, we will not further expand such flows that contain another occurrence of either $a$ or $b$. This means that, in fact, any implementation choice that renders the obtained flow recursive, is not expanded further. The number of EX-flows rooted at $a$ that contain no (mutual) recursion within them is finite, and the algorithm is thus guaranteed to halt. Similarly, whenever we compute the top-j flow rooted at $a$, the only flows rooted at $a$ that we attempt to use as sub-flows are those already computed, and the algorithm is thus guaranteed to halt.

2. We have shown above (Theorem 3.16) that the basic $A^*$-like algorithm inserts flows to $Out$ in a correct order. Algorithm TOP-K inserts flows to $Out$ at the same order as the basic algorithm, except for the case where flows are put in the $OnHold$ queue. However, recall that flows put in $OnHold$ are those that violate a constraint of Lemma 3.18. Thus, there exists, at each point, a top-j flow that is not one of those put in $OnHold$, and this flow is found by the algorithm following Theorem 3.16. Note that the flows that are put in $OnHold$ may be parts of lower-ranked flows, and are thus returned to Frontier for further computation (line 9 of Algorithm HandleFullFlow).

□

*Complexity*    We next provide a worst-case complexity analysis of the algorithm, as follows.

**Theorem 3.22**    Given a BP specification $s$ (with $cWeight$ and $aggr$) and a number $k$, the time complexity of refinedFindFlows in Algorithm TOP-K is $O(|s|^3 * k)$.

***Proof.*** The number of entries in $FTable$ is $k * |s|$. Now, for each flow node $v$ considered during the course of the algorithm execution, either it already appears in $FTable$, or it does not. The case where the sub-flow requested for $v$ does not appear in the table may only happen $k * |s|$ times, while computing the top-k flows rooted at $v$. The cost of computation for such cases is $O(|s|)$ for searching the table, (assuming that we have an index that allows, in O(1) time, to get the worst ranked entry for a given row; otherwise there may be an additional factor of $k$) and then $O(1)$ of additional computation, considering direct expansions of $v$, a total of $O(k * |s|^2)$.

If the sub-flow considered for $v$ does already appears in $FTable$, we only need to point the implementation of $v$ to the sub-flow that was already computed ($O(1)$). We next consider the number of times that this scenario may occur.

We start by considering the computation of top-1 flows. Now, consider some activity name $a$. Say that we have encountered some node $n$ with activity name $a$, and then, before we are done computing the top-1 flow rooted at $n$, we have encountered, at another point of the search tree, another node $n'$ with label $a$. The course of the algorithm execution follows observation 2 above: it suspends the computation for the top-1 flow of $n'$, until computation of the top-1 flow of $n$ is done (by putting $n'$ "on hold," line 10 of Algorithm refinedHandleExps. The number of such suspensions, while computing the top-1 flow of $n$, is bounded by the size of the specification $s$, for each such $n$. The same argument holds for computation of the $i$'th highest weighted flow, for each $i = 1, ..., k$, leading to a total bounded by $O(k * |s|^3)$ for this case. The overall time complexity is thus polynomial in $|s|$ and $k$.    $\square$

Similar arguments can be used to show an additional characteristic of the algorithm that may be thought of as the analog of the notion of *polynomial delay* [Read and Tarjan, 1975].

**Theorem 3.23**    The delay between inserting the $i$-th and the $(i + 1)$-th result to $Out$ is polynomial in $|s|$.

**Proof.** Note that Algorithm refinedFindFlows computes flows in an *incremental manner*: to compute the $i + 1$-th ranked, we start from the flow that appears first in $Frontier$, after computing the $i$-th ranked flow; for this flow, we try expansions that were not previously used (line 8 of refinedHandleExps). The complexity of computation of the $i + 1$-th ranked flow, given the $i$-th ranked flow (i.e., the delay) is obviously polynomial in $|s|$ and in $k$: this follows from the incremental nature of computation, combined with Thm. 3.22. It remains to show that the delay is in fact *independent of $k$*. Similarly, to above, we assume the existence of an index that allows, in O(1) time, to retrieve (pointer to) the point at the table containing the highest ranked un-handled flows appearing in a given row of $FTable$ (such index may be implemented). At each stage, we only need to consider the highest ranked such un-handled flow (line 13), and thus never consider flows computed in steps earlier than the last step for every activity name. This number is thus bounded by $|s|$ and independent of $k$.    $\square$

The last part of Algorithm TOP-K involves the invocation of EnumerateFlows that outputs the top-k flows. Recall that the size of a single flow in this set may be exponential in the BP specification size (even in the absence of recursion), and thus one cannot expect an enumeration algorithm that is polynomial in the BP specification size. However, it is easy to observe that the complexity of EnumerateFlows is linear in the *output* size, as it simply follows pointers to materialize each output EX-flow.

### 3.3.3    HISTORY-DEPENDENT WEIGHTS

So far we have assumed that the $cWeight$ function given as input is history-independent, i.e., the $cWeight$ of each implementation choice is the same for every occurrence of the corresponding compound activity. As explained above, this is often not the case in practice. We next discuss the two additional classes of $cWeight$ functions defined above, and consider the adaptation of our top-k algorithm to account for these classes.

First, we may show that if $cWeight$ may be unbounded-history, then there exists no correct algorithm for TOP-K-FLOWS. To that end, we define the decision problem of BEST-FLOW, which tests, given a weighted BP specification $s$, and a threshold $t$, whether there exists an EX-flow in $flows(s)$ whose $fWeight$ is greater than $t$.

**Theorem 3.24**    If the $cWeight$ function given as input may be unbounded-history, then BEST−FLOW is undecidable.

**Proof.** The proof is by a reduction from the *halting problem*. Given a Turing Machine $M$, the idea is to "encode" $M$ using the BP specification. The states of $M$ are represented by activity names; implementations model the transitions between states, as well as changes to the tape and to the head location; and the history of flow is utilized to allow "read" operations from the tape.

More formally, given a Turing Machine $M$ with a set of states $Q$, an initial state $q_0 \in Q$, an accepting state $q_F \in Q$, a tape alphabet $\Gamma$ and a transition function $\delta$, we generate a BP specification whose set of compound activity names corresponds to $Q$, and additionally it contains an atomic activity $a$. The implementations set of each compound activity corresponding to a state $a$, contains a single-node implementation for each activity name $a'$ (possibly $= a$) such that there is a transition from $a$ to $a'$ according to $\delta$. The $cWeight$ value of the formula $f$ guarding each such implementation is dictated by the preceding flow $e$, and $\delta$; $cWeight(e, f) = 1$ if and only if, when following, in $M$, the transitions dictated by the EX-flow $e$, the symbol under the tape head is $b$, and $\delta(a, b) = a'$ (meaning that there exists a transition from state $a$ to state $a'$ given that the symbol $b$ is under the tape head). Otherwise, $cWeight(e, f) = 0$. As $cWeight$ function is unbounded-history, it is allowed to determine its value according to the entire preceding flow. For the accepting state, its single implementation consist of the atomic activity $a$, with $cWeight$ of 1. We use multiplication for aggregation, and seek for full flows with $cWeight$ higher than 0. An accepting flow of such $cWeight$ exists if and only if there exists an accepting run of the TM.    □

Fortunately, recall that in practical cases the $cWeight$ function is in fact bounded-history. In the sequel we consider such bounded-history $cWeight$ functions, and explain how to adapt our top-k algorithm to weighted BPs with such weight functions.

First, we introduce the notion of *partial tracing system* for BP specifications. These notions were introduced by Deutch and Milo [2008], and we use it here as auxiliary tools for query evaluation. We use the term EX-traces to refer to the execution traces that are the results of logging execution flows. Then, we define semi-naive EX-traces. These are traces obtained through the use of a tracing system that applies a "mask," i.e., a renaming function on activities names occurring in the EX-flow. More concretely we have the following.

**Definition 3.25    [Semi-naive EX-traces]** Given a BP specification $s$ and a renaming function $\pi$ from activity names in $s$ to activity names in $\mathcal{A}$, the set of *semi-naive* EX-traces defined by $s$ and $\pi$, denoted $semiNaive(s, \pi)$, consists of all the EX-traces $e$ obtained from the naive EX-traces $e' \in Naive(s)$ by replacing each label $a$ in $e'$ by $\pi(a)$.

Semi-naive EX-traces can be viewed as the BP analog of XML trees defined by *DTDs with specialization* [Papakonstantinou and Vianu, 2000]. In both cases the node labels give only partial information about the origin of the node (the corresponding BP activity, for EX-traces, or the DTD type, for XML trees).

**Theorem 3.26**    Given a weighted BP specification $s$ with bounded-history $cWeight$ function (with bound $b$), and given also a number $k$, top-k(s) can be computed in time polynomial w.r.t. $|s|$, $k$, and the output size, and exponential w.r.t. $b$.

To prove the theorem, we next explain the revised top-k algorithm that accounts for bounded-history $cWeight$ functions.

**Revised algorithm—general framework**    Algorithm TOP-K depicted above has assumed that the $cWeight$ function is history-independent. To account for history-dependent functions, we shall utilize the notion of semi-naive tracing as a tool. In particular, we define the notion of a weighted BP specification with semi-Naive tracing *capturing* a given set of EX-flows. This notion will be useful in the sequel.

**Definition    3.27**    A    weighted    BP    specification    $s$    (and    weight    functions $(cWeight, aggr, fWeight)$) along with a renaming function $\pi$ over its activities *captures* a (possibly infinite) set of EX-flows $T$, with respect to a weight function $(cWeight', aggr', fWeight')$ over $T$ if:

1. semi-naive$(s, \pi) = T$, i.e., for each $t \in$ semi-naive$(s, \pi)$ there exists $e \in T$ such that $t = e^4$, and vice versa, i.e., for each $e \in T$ there exists $t \in$ semi-naive$(s, \pi)$ such that $t = e$; and

2. $\forall_{e \in flows(s)} fWeight(e) = \Delta(\Pi(e))$ where $\Pi(e) \in T$ is obtained from $e$ by replacing each activity name $a$ in $e$ by $\pi(a)$.

The BOUNDED-TOP-K algorithm, computing top-k flows for weighted BP specifications with bounded-history $cWeight$ functions, then operates in two steps.

1. The first step of the algorithm, namely Algorithm COMPILE-HISTORY-INDEPENDENT, compiles, given a weighted BP $s$ with a bounded-history $cWeight$ function (and a $fWeight$ function), a weighted BP $s'$ with a history-independent $cWeight$ function, and a renaming function $\pi$, such that $s', \pi$ captures $flows(s)$ (w.r.t. $fWeight$).

2. The second step of the algorithm, namely Algorithm SEMI-NAIVE-TOP-K is an adaptation of Algorithm TOP-K, applied to find the top-k semi-naive EX-traces of $s', \pi$.

Next, we explain both steps.

---

[4]This equality is an equality between EX-flows, corresponding to a node-label, edge-relation and guarding formulas preserving isomorphism.

**Algorithm** `COMPILE-HISTORY-INDEPENDENT`    Given a weighted BP specification $s$ with activities $a_1, \ldots, a_n$, and weight functions $(cWeight, aggr, fWeight)$, s.t. $cWeight$ is bounded-history, denote the history bound of $cWeight$ by $b$. We generate a new weighted BP specification $s'$, with renaming function $\pi$ and history-independent $cWeight'$, such that $s'$ along with $\pi$ capture $flows(s)$ with correct weights. The different components of $s', \pi$ are as follows.

- Activities Names. The activities names in $s'$ are tuples of the form $(a, pre = [pre_1^1, \ldots, pre_n^1, \ldots, pre_1^m, \ldots, pre_n^m], post = [post_1^1, \ldots, post_n^1, \ldots, post_1^m \ldots post_n^m])$ where $a$ is an activity name, $pre_j^i$ denotes a formula guarding the implementation chosen for $a_i$ in its previous $j$ expansions, prior to expanding $a$, and $post_j^i$ denotes a formula guaranteed to guard the implementation chosen for $a_i$ in its next $j$ expansions. The idea is that $pre$ encodes all information required for computing $cWeight$ of $a$'s guarding formulas, and $post$ encodes all information required for activities that follow $a$ in the flow. We use $pre_j^i = \bot$ if $a_i$ was not expanded $j$ steps before the flow reaches $a$, and $post_j^i = \bot$ if $a_i$ will not be expanded $j$ times before the execution of $a$ terminates.

- Guarding Formulas and Weight Function. Let $f_1, \ldots, f_l$ be the guarding formulas appearing in $s$, then guarding formulas in $s'$ are of the form $(f_i, pre)$ where $pre$ is a vector of formulas of size $b$. The $cWeight'$ function is defined as $cWeight'(f_i, pre) = cWeight(f_{pre}, f_i)$ where $f_{pre}$ is some arbitrary partial EX-flow of $s$ for which the next node to be expanded is guarded by $f_i$, and in which the last implementation were guarded by the sequence of formulas in $pre$[5]. For aggregation, $aggr' = aggr$, and the obtained flow weight function is called $fWeight'$.

- Implementation Function. Next we construct the implementations of $(a, pre, post)$ in $s'$. For each implementation $F_i$ of $a$ in $s$ (guarded by $f_i$), we create a set of new implementations, all guarded by $f_i$. Each implementation is obtained by annotating each activity $b$ in $F_i$ with vectors of pre and post conditions. The construction is as follows: (a) if $r$ is the root of an implementation $F_i$ of $(a, pre_a, post_a)$ guarded by $f_i$ (note that many such activity names are created for any activity name $a$, differing in their pre- and post-condition vectors), then the pre-condition of $r$ is obtained from $pre_a$, shifted by one step, recording $F_i$ (and possibly deleting some formula from the vector, if reached the bound); (b) if there exists an edge from some node $n$ to some node $n'$ in $F_i$, the post-condition annotating $n$ complies with the pre-condition annotating $n'$; and (c) if $e$ is the end node of $F_i$, the post-condition annotating it complies with $post_a$.

- Renaming Function. We define $\pi(a, pre, post) = a$ for each activity name $(a, pre, post)$.

In what follows, let $\Pi$ be a renaming function over flows, where $\Pi(e)$ is $e'$ obtained from $e$ by replacing every activity name $a$ in $e$ by $\pi(a)$. We claim that $s', \pi$ constructed by the algorithm capture $flows(s)$, with respect to $fWeight$. To observe that this holds, first note that

---

[5]This weight is uniquely defined, since $cWeight$ has an history bound of $b$.

every implementation of $a' = (a, pre, post)$ in $s'$ was obtained from an implementation of $a$ in $s$ by replacing all activity names $b$ in this implementation by some activity names $b, pre', post'$. Thus, by applying $\Pi$ over the corresponding implementation of $a'$ one obtains every possible implementation of $a$, and only such implementations, i.e., semi-naive$(s', \pi) = flows(s)$. As for weight of flows, let $e \in flows(s)$ and let $e' \in flows(s')$ such that $\Pi(e') = e$. We next show, by induction on the size of $e$, that $fWeight(e) = fWeight'(e')$: for the induction basis, a flow consisting only of the root activity of $s$ $(s')$ has a weight of $1_{aggr} = 1_{aggr'}$; now, assume that $fWeight(e_1) = fWeight'(e'_1)$ for $e_1$ $(e'_1)$ that bears exactly the same structure as $e$ $(e')$ except for its last implementation choice. Then this last implementation bears, in $s$, a weight of $aggr(fWeight(e_1), cWeight(e_1, f)$ where $f$ is its guarding formula. The corresponding implementation in $s'$ bears a weight of $aggr(fWeight'(e'_1), cWeight((f, pre)))$ where $pre$ is the $pre$ vector encoded within the activity in $e'_1$ whose implementation was chosen to form $e$. But $cWeight(e_1, f) = cWeight((f, pre))$, because the algorithm construction of the implementation function defines a pre-condition vector that is consistent with the sequence of implementation choices made in the course of the flow (in this case $e_1$).

This concludes the description of Algorithm COMPILE-HISTORY-INDEPENDENT.

**Algorithm** SEMI-NAIVE-TOP-K   The second part of the algorithm finds the top-k EX-traces defined by $(s', \pi')$. Recall that $s'$ is history-independent, and a naive solution would attempt to apply Algorithm TOP-K, as is, over $s'$, to find its top-k EX-flows; then apply $\Pi'$ [6] over each such EX-flow to obtain the top-k EX-traces of $(s', \pi')$ which are also the top-k EX-flows of $s$. The crux here is that distinct EX-flows of $s$ may be mapped by $\Pi'$ to the same EX-trace, thus this algorithm may fail to find $k$ distinct EX-traces.

Instead, we revise the algorithm as follows. Recall that Algorithm TOP-K makes use of an $FTable$ whose rows correspond to activity names and whose columns are marked 1 to k. We maintain an additional "shadow" table $STable$, in which every row corresponds to an activity name $b = \pi(a)$ where $a$ is an activity of $s'$, and its columns are marked 1 to k*$N(b)$, where $N(b)$ is the number of distinct activity names mapped by $\pi$ to $b$. We now execute Algorithm TOP-K on $s'$, but whenever the algorithm adds a (sub-)flow $e'$ to $FTable$, at a row corresponding to an activity $a$ of $s'$, we add $\Pi(e')$ at the appropriate location (according to its weight), in the row of $\pi(a)$ at $STable$. We further change the pointer, set by TOP-K to point at the entry in $FTable$, to point to the newly added entry in $STable$. This pointer will be used for checking whether a sub-flow rooted at $a$ was used within a computed EX-flow (Line 9 of Algorithm refinedHandleExps) as well as in the flow enumeration (Algorithm EnumerateFlows).

**Complexity**   The complexity of Algorithm COMPILE-HISTORY-INDEPENDENT is polynomial in the BP specification size $|s|$ and exponential in the history bound $b$, as each constructed activity name is composed out of a single activity name in $s$ and a vector of guarding formulas, of size $b$. The complexity of Algorithm SEMI-NAIVE-TOP-K is polynomial in $k$, in the size of its input $|s'|$, in the

---

[6] $\Pi'(e)$ is obtained from $e$ by replacing each activity name $a$ in $e$ by $\pi'(a)$.

size of its output and in $max_a N(a)$ where $a$ is an activity name and $N(a)$ is the number of distinct activity names mapped by $\pi$ to $a$. In our case $|s'|$ is polynomial in the BP specification size $|s|$ and exponential in the history bound $b$, and $max_a N(a)$ is exponential in $b$ (as all activity names of the form $(a, pre, post)$ are mapped to $a$, and their number equals the number of distinct such $pre$ and $post$ vectors, in turn exponential in $b$).

This concludes the proof of Theorem 3.26.

We further show that this exponential dependency on the history size is inevitable, as the following theorem holds (recall that BEST-FLOW is the decision problem corresponding to TOP-K-FLOWS, i.e., is the problem of deciding the existence of an EX-flow of the given BP specification, whose weight is greater than some given bound).

**Theorem 3.28**   For bounded-history $cWeight$ functions with bound $b$, BEST-FLOW is NP-hard in $b$.

*Proof.* We use a reduction from Set Cover. Given an instance of set cover, namely a set $X = \{X_1, ..., X_n\}$ of items, a set of subsets $S = \{S_1, ..., S_m\}$ and a bound $B$, we construct a BP as follows: its activity names are $S_0$ (root), $S_1, ..., S_m$ (compound) and $a$ (atomic). Each $S_i$ ($i = 0, ..., m$) bears $2 * m + 1$ implementations: for each $j = 1, ..., m$, $S_i$ has two implementations, each consisting of a single node whose activity name is $S_j$: the first is guarded by a formula "$\$S_i$ = chosen," and the second by "$\$S_i$ = not chosen;" the last implementation of $S_i$, guarded by "$\$S_i$ = done," consists of a single node whose activity name is $a$. The $cWeight$ of "$\$S_i$ = chosen" and of "$\$S_i$ = not chosen" is 1, and that of "$\$S_i$ = done" depends on the last $B$ choices: it is 1 if and only if the set of $S_i$ sets for which "$\$S_i$ = chosen," within these last $B$ choices, covers $X$. Otherwise, its $cWeight$ is also 0. We use multiplication for $aggr$. It is easy to observe that there exists an EX-flow of $fWeight$ greater than 0.5 if and only if there exists a set cover of size smaller than $B$. (The EX-flow consists of an implementation choice guarded by "$\$S_i$ = chosen" for each $S_i$ in the cover, and "$\$S_i$ = not chosen" for each $S_i$ not in the cover).

□

### 3.3.4   FROM IDENTIFYING TOP-K FLOWS TO EVALUATING SELECTION QUERIES

So far we have only considered the identification of top-k EX-flows of a given BP specification, without considering a pattern that these flows should conform to. We will next show how to use an algorithm that computes the top-k flows, as a black box for the evaluation of top-k selection queries.

We employ a two-step algorithm, as follows.

1. The first step is a query evaluation algorithm SELECT-FLOWS (detailed below) that, given a BP specification $s$ and an EX-pattern $p$, constructs a BP specification $s'$, including only those EX-flows of $s$ that qualify according to $p$. Intuitively, $s'$ is the "intersection" of $s$ with $p$.

2. The second algorithm is our TOP-K algorithm, that retrieves the top-k EX-flows of the constructed $s'$.

We next detail Algorithm SELECT-FLOWS for the first step.

SELECT-FLOWS   We construct a BP $s' = (S', s'_0, \tau')$ that is intuitively the "intersection" of the original BP $s = (S, s_0, \tau)$ with the query $q$. We next explain how this $s'$ is constructed.

First, consider queries without transitive nodes or edges. Let $n_s \in s$ and $n_q \in q$ be two nodes sharing the same (compound) activity name $a$. We define a new activity name $[n_q, n_s, a]$. Note that a node $n_q$ (resp. $n_s$) of the pattern $q$ (BP $s$) may appear in several such new activities $[n_q, n_s^i, a]$ (resp. $[n_q^i, n_s, a]$).

For compound (non-transitive) activities, the implementation $\tau'$ of $[n_q, n_s, a]$ consists of all possible *direct* implementations of $n_s$ in $s$ in which there exist embeddings of the *direct* implementation of $n_q$ in $q$. In the resulting graph (for each of the possible embeddings) are labeled by triplets, as above, recording for every activity pair in $p$, to which activity pair in $s$ it was mapped in the given embedding (if at all, otherwise the node simply keeps its original identifier). If no embedding was found, $[n_q, n_s, a]$ is marked as failure. The embeddings may be found using conventional algorithms for subgraph homomorphism.

As a final step, the algorithm performs "garbage collection" by recursively marking as failure activities for which all possible implementations contain failure activities, and then removing from $s'$ all DAGs that contain failure such activities.

When the query contains transitive edges, we also define new activity name for every transitive edge $e_q \in q$ and activity $n_s \in s$. When the pattern sub-graphs are embedded into the BP, the transitive edges $e_q \in q$ (that connect two pattern nodes) are mapped to all possible paths in the BP (connecting the two corresponding BP nodes). In the output graph, a BP node $n_s$ (with label $a$) that appear on such path is labeled by the triplet $[e_q, n_s, a]$.

Finally, when $q$ contains transitive activities, the algorithm becomes somewhat more complex. Recall that transitive activities allow to navigate (transitively) inside the compound activities and query their internal flow at any depth of nesting. Specifically, part of the direct implementation of $n_q$ can be matched with the direct implementation of $n_s$, while other parts may be matched at deeper levels of the implementation. To account for that, the algorithm considers all possible splits of the query into sub-queries, and the embeddings of those into the DAGs in $s$, and then proceeds for each split as described above.

*Complexity*   The complexity of the first algorithm is $|s|^{|p|}$ where the exponential dependency on $|p|$ is due to the need to consider matches of the pattern o the specification. This is also a bound on the size of the resulting BP $s'$. The second step, as shown above, is then polynomial in the size of its input $s'$, and in $k$, thus the PTIME data complexity remains.

## 3.4   EVALUATION OF PROJECTION QUERIES UNDER *MAX* SEMANTICS

We next discuss evaluation algorithms for top-k *projection* queries, where the results are ranked based on the *max* semantics (*sum* semantics is discussed in the following section). We first show that a direct adaptation of the selection queries evaluation algorithm) to projection queries, fails at achieving a PTIME query evaluation algorithm, and finally describe an alternative algorithm that overcomes this.

*History-independence assumption.*   Again, and for the remainder of this book, we will assume that the *cWeight* function is history independent; otherwise, we first use Algorithm COMPILE-HISTORY-INDEPENDENT to generate a BP specification with an history-independent *cWeight* function, then employ the relevant algorithm for the history-independent case.

*First attempt—explicit enumeration of EX-flows.*   The first simple approach for evaluating projection queries is to first treat the query as a selection query, and use Algorithm TOP-K-SELECTION to explicitly enumerate the flows of $s$ satisfying the query, along with their $fWeight$ values (If multiple flows lead to the same projection result, one may need to generate the top-$k'$ flows for some $k' > k$, leading to $k$ distinct projection results.) Next, for each obtained flow, we may compute the result of projecting it on the EX-pattern projection part. Each projection result is ranked based on the maximal fWeight of a flow leading to it.

Note, however, that this naive algorithm may incur time that is exponential in the BP specification size, as well as in the output size, as the following theorem holds.

**Theorem 3.29**   There exists a fixed-sized query $q$ such that for every natural number $n$ there exists a BP specification $s_n$ whose size is linear in $n$, such that even the smallest size of any EX-flow of $q(s_n)$ is exponential in $n$, while the size of the largest EX-flow in $q_\downarrow(s_n)$ is bounded by a constant.

**Proof.**   Consider a BP specification in which each activity has a single implementation, as follows: the implementation of each activity $a_i$ ($i = 1, ..., n-1$) consists of two nodes labeled $a_{i+1}$, and the implementation of $a_n$ consists of a single atomic activity. Consider also a query that looks for the root activity node, with (indirect) implementation consisting of two *any*-labeled nodes. These two nodes are connected by a transitive edge. The query then projects over the root node. It is easy to observe that $q(s_n) = s_n$, and it has only a single possible EX-flow. The size of this flow (containing two instances of $a_2$, 4 instances of $a_3$, etc.) is exponential in $n$. Note that in contrast, $q_\downarrow(s_n)$ consists of a single activity pair.   □

*Second attempt—Computing a compact representation of all projections.*   An alternative approach to adapting the selection query evaluation algorithm follows the idea of generating a BP specification $s'$ along with a renaming function $\pi'$, that captures all results, namely $q_\downarrow(s)$, and then retrieving the top-k out of these. Unfortunately, this approach would also lead to an infeasible algorithm, as there exist no such $s'$, $\pi'$ s.t. $s'$ is of size polynomial in $s$.

Next, we show an alternative, PTIME, algorithm for evaluating top-k projection queries. As shown above, it is infeasible to compute a compact representation that captures *all* projection results (in the sense of Definition 3.27) and then retrieve the top-k results out of them. However, we may still perform a two-steps algorithm, similar to TOP-K-SELECTIONS. However, instead of a first step that generates a BP specification capturing the *entire* set of results $q_\downarrow(s)$, the first step of the refined evaluation algorithm generates a specification that captures only a *subset* of $q_\downarrow(s)$, including in particular the top-k weighted projections. We say that such BP *k-captures* $q_\downarrow(s)$. Formally, we have the following.

**Definition 3.30**   Given two weighted BP specifications $s'$, $s$, a renaming function $\pi'$ mapping activities names in $s'$ to activities names in $s$, a query $q$, and a number $k$, we say that $s'$ *k-captures* $q_\downarrow(s)$ if $top-k(q_\downarrow, s) \subseteq \pi'(flows(s')) \subseteq q_\downarrow(s)$ (overloading notations, $\pi'(E) = \{\pi'(e)|e \in E\}$), and the *score* of each projection is the same as the $fWeight$ of the corresponding flow of $s'$.

The following theorem holds.

**Theorem 3.31**   Given a weighted BP specification $s$ and a projection query $q = (p, P)$, we may compute a weighted BP specification $s'$ (and a renaming function $\pi'$) that *k-captures* $q_\downarrow(s)$ in time polynomial in $s$, with the exponent determined by the query size.

*Proof.* We present an evaluation algorithm, named Algorithm K-CAPTURES, whose output is a BP specification $s'$, weight functions for the flows of $s'$ (denoted $cWeight'$, $aggr'$ and $fWeight'$), and a renaming function $\pi'$ over the activity names of $s'$, that *k-captures* $q_\downarrow(s)$. Algorithm K-CAPTURES operates in the same way as the Algorithm for selection queries evaluation, except for the treatment of transitive queries described next.

The end-nodes of each transitive edge are matched by the algorithm to specification nodes (denote these as $n$ for the start node of the edge and $m$ for the end node), and it remains to consider the paths in-between them. If the transitive edge does not appear in the projection part, we only need to verify that a path exists, as in the Algorithm for selection queries.

Otherwise, when the transitive edge does appear in the projection part, then each projection result contains a path, to which the edge is matched. It is infeasible to create an implementation for each distinct projection (i.e., each distinct path), as the number of paths between two nodes of the specification may be exponential in the specification size. Fortunately, we are only interested in the top-k projections, in which *only the top-k paths may appear*. We thus design a Dynamic Programming algorithm, namely TOP-K-PATHS (explained next), returning a BP specification whose possible EX-flows are exactly the top-k paths from $n$ to $m$ (along with their correct weights). TOP-K-PATHS is then employed whenever the algorithm encounters a transitive edge.

*Note*   We assume in the sequel that the transitive edge appears within an implementation of a transitive node. If not, then any $k$ [7] paths may be chosen, as they all co-appear in the same implementation, thus share the same weight.

*TOP-K-PATHS*   First, we assign a unique identifier to each specification node, then generate a new set of nodes $[n_j, i]$ for each $n_j$ of the specification and for each $i = 1, ..., k$, and initialize a table which keeps track of the $i$'th most likely path from each $n_j$ to $m$, along with its weight. When the table is full, it contains in particular the top-k paths from $n$ to $m$, which are explicitly generated.

To fill in the table, we use the auxiliary notion of *children*, as follows. We say that $n_2$ is a child of $n_1$ if there is an edge from $n_1$ to $n_2$, or if $n_1$ is a activation node of a compound activity and $n_2$ is a start node of its implementation, or if $n_2$ is an completion node of a compound activity and $n_1$ is an end-node of its implementation.

The computation of values in the table proceeds as follows, computing the $i$'th paths for increasing values of $i$. When computing the top-$i$ path originating at some node $l$, we consider all *children* of $l$ in the specification. For each such child $u$, say that $j$ is the greatest index of a path originating in $u$ that was used as a sub-path in some $r < i$ ranked path of $l$ that was previously computed. Then we compute the $j + 1$ path originated in $u$ (if it was not already computed), and obtain $score(u)$, the score of $u$ as a candidate for the path being generated for $l$. In case the edge between $l$ and $u$ is a zoom-in edge, $score(u)$ is aggregated with the $cWeight$ of $f$, where $f$ is the formula guarding the implementation rooted at $u$. The child of $u$ with the maximal score, along with its corresponding sub-path, is chosen for the top-$i$ path originating at $l$.

Each obtained path serves as a separate implementation of the corresponding compound activity.

*The renaming function $\pi'$*   The renaming function $\pi'$ is simply designed as $\pi'([a, q']) = a$ for each sub-query $q'$, and $\pi'([a, i]) = a$ for each $i = 1, ..., k$.

The following lemma holds.

**Lemma 3.32**

  *The BP specification generated by Algorithm* TOP-K-PATHS *captures the k highest weighted paths from n to m.*

**Proof.** The proof is by induction on $i$. For $i = 1$, the lemma trivially holds (the best path consists of the best implementation for the start node, along with the best path originating at any of its children). Now assume correctness for $i = k$. That is, the $k$'th ranked path contains only the $p_1 \leq k$ best implementation of $l$, and the $p_2 \leq k$ best implementation of some child. The $k + 1$ ranked path obviously uses, at worst, the $p_1 + 1$ best implementation of its origin. As for the children, if it has the same son as the $k$'th ranked path then it obviously uses its $p_2 + 1$ best ranked path; if it uses the $p_2'$ ranked path of some other child, then assume by contradiction that $p_2' > k + 1$. Then

---

[7]If there are only $k' < k$ paths, then all are matched.

there are at least $k + 1$ better paths obtained by improving the path originated at the chosen child, in contradiction to the path being ranked $k + 1$.    □

*Complexity*   Note first that for each activity node occurring in $s$ there are at most $2^{|q|}$ activities mapped to it by $\pi'$. Further note (Observation 2 above) that an EX-flow that is one of the top-k EX-flows of $s$, contains at most $k$ recursive invocations of each activity. This means that in total the number of EX-flows of $s'$ mapped to the same EX-flow is bounded by $|s| * 2^{|q|} * k$. The complexity of the above algorithm is thus polynomial in the BP size $s$ and in $k$, with the exponent determined by the query size $q$. The exponential dependency on the query size is due to the algorithm for transitive nodes, considering all query splits, as well as due to the embedding algorithm whose complexity is exponential in the size of the sub-query matched.

□

**Corollary 3.33**
    *We may compute* $top − k(q_\downarrow, s)$ *in time polynomial in the size of the BP and in the output size, and exponential in the query size.*

**Proof.** The algorithm, namely `TOP-K-PROJECTIONS`, first applies Algorithm `K-CAPTURES` given in the proof of Theorem 3.31, to obtain $s'$, $\pi'$ that k-capture $q_\downarrow(s)$. The flows of $s'$ capture all results of top-k$(q_\downarrow, s)$, but possibly some additional flows. Then, `TOP-K-PROJECTIONS` applies finds the $k$-highest weighted semi-naive EX-traces of $s'$, $\pi'$ as described above. The time complexity of both steps is polynomial in the size of the input BP specification and exponential in the query size, and so is the complexity of Algorithm `TOP-K-PROJECTIONS`.    □

So far, we have discussed the computation of a weight of a sub-flow (for evaluation of projection queries) according to a particular *max* semantics, where the weight of a sub-flow is defined as the maximal weight of an EX-flow containing it. Particularly in the context of weights that reflect *probability* of executions, a different semantic that is of interest is one where the weight (probability) of a sub-flow is defined as the *sum* of weights (probabilities) of full flows containing it.

The *sum* semantics is a common semantics for projection queries in probabilistic settings, employed also for probabilistic XML and probabilistic relational databases (e.g., [Foster et al., 2008; Senellart and Abiteboul, 2007; Suciu et al., 2011]). Yet, we show below that in the BP context it makes query evaluation *computationally much harder*, compared to *max* semantics (NP-hard and EXPTIME vs. the PTIME of Deutch and Milo [2009a,b]). Intuitively, this is because the computation now has to implicitly compute sum-of-probabilities over all relevant flows (and there may be infinitely many).

**Restriction to a probabilistic model.** As explained above, the *sum* semantics has a particularly appealing interpretation when weights are not general, but rather reflect *probabilities*. We therefore focus in the sequel on this particular case. Generalizing the results of this section to a general

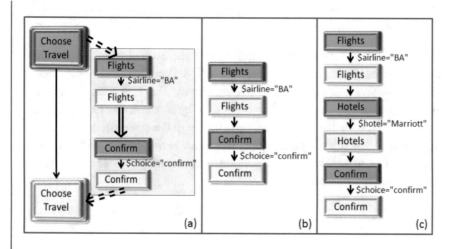

**Figure 3.4:** Query.

weighted model may be possible, but has not yet been done. We note that in this case, instead of arbitrary choice and flow *weight*, we in fact have in hand choice *likelihood*. To make the restriction to probabilities explicit, we abandon the notations cWeight and fWeight, and instead use *c-likelihood* and *f-likelihood* to denote choice and flow likelihood, respectively. Similarly, instead of referring to weighted BPs, we refer in this context to *probabilistic BPs*.

**Boolean queries.** Before we can study projection queries under the *sum* semantics, we need to turn to an auxiliary tool, namely boolean queries. The semantics of boolean queries in the probabilistic setting is the expected one: the probability that a boolean query holds is the sum of probabilities of the EX-flows that satisfy it.

Consequently, the next section is devoted to the evaluation of *boolean* queries, and the one that follows focuses on *projection* queries, both with respect to the *sum* semantics.

## 3.5   EVALUATION OF BOOLEAN QUERIES

As explained above, boolean queries are important tools for the evaluation of projection queries with sum semantics. We next define the semantics of boolean queries on probabilistic BPs.

**Query Result.** We say that an EX-flow $e$ satisfies a boolean query $p$ (denoted $p(e) = true$), if there exists an embedding of $p$ in $e$. Given a BP specification $s$, the probability that a random EX-flow of $s$ satisfies $p$ is the sum of likelihoods of EX-flows satisfying $p$, namely

$$likelihood^b(p, s) = \sum \{\Delta(e) \mid e \in flows(s) \wedge p(e) = true\},$$

where $\Delta$ is the f–likelihood function for $s$. When $s$ is clear from context we omit it and use $likelihood^b(p)$.

**Example 3.34**    Reconsider our travel agency BP specification (Figure 2.5), accompanied by Table 3.2 that describes the likelihoods of value assignments for the different variables affecting the BP execution, and consequently the c–likelihood function for the guarding formulas. Consider also the query in Figure 3.4(a), but assume first, for simplicity, that the edge between `Flights` and `Confirm` is a regular one, rather than transitive. Observe that, still, this query has an infinite number of possible satisfying EX-flows, differing, for example, in what the user had done prior to the reservation. The infinite number of options is due to the fact that the user may make some selections and reset, then make other selections and reset, an unbounded number of times before making her final (confirmed) selection. The query likelihood is the sum of likelihoods of all these flows; to compute it, we define a variable $x$ reflecting the likelihood of a query match. Intuitively, $x$ is the probability that the query is matched in the first reservation choice of the user, or that the user resets and a match is obtained in a following reservation choice. Thus,

$$x = c-likelihood(\$searchType = \text{``}flightsOnly\text{''}) * c-likelihood(\$airline = \text{``}BA\text{''}) *$$
$$c-likelihood(\$choice = \text{``}confirm\text{''}) + c-likelihood(\$choice = \text{``}reset\text{''}) * x.$$

Namely, $x = 0.5 * 0.7 * 0.2 + 0.6 * x$. Thus, $x = 0.175$.

We have assumed above that the edge connecting `Flights` and `Confirm` is non-transitive. If the edge is transitive, the computation becomes more complex, accounting for all possible paths in-between `Flights` and `Confirm`. We discuss such computations below.

We refer to the problem of computing $likelihood^b(p, s)$, given a boolean query $p$ and a BP specification $s$, as `BOOL-EVAL`, and to the problem of approximating it up to any given $\epsilon$ as `APPROX-BOOL-EVAL`.

First, we may show that `BOOL-EVAL` may not be solved in the general case, as the following theorem holds.

**Theorem 3.35**    $likelihood^b(p, s)$ may be irrational, even if all likelihoods in $s$ are rational and $p$ contains no transitive nodes and edges.

**_Proof._** The proof follows directly from results of Etessami and Yannakakis [2009] that presents a Recursive Markov Chain (RMC) $m$, with rational probabilities, where the probability for execution termination is irrational. We construct a BP specification $s$ with structure similar to $m$ and a boolean query $p$ that is satisfied by all terminating execution (i.e., the probability of the query to be satisfied is the probability of obtaining a full EX-flow).

The BP specification $s$ has a root DAG with a single activity $r$, having 3 possible implementations: the first, with c–likelihood of $\frac{1}{6}$, is a chain, of length 5, with all activities labeled by $r$.

The second contains a single atomic activity node, labeled by $a$, and its c–likelihood is $\frac{1}{3}$, and the third contains a single compound activity node $A$. $A$ has a single recursive implementation, i.e., an implementation of c–likelihood 1 consisting of a single $A$-labeled node. The EX-pattern $p$ seeks for EX-flows with root activity $r$ (namely $p$ consists of a single activity pair, labeled $r$). It is thus satisfied by all the full EX-flows of $s$, or in other words, by all terminating executions. $likelihood^b(p, s)$ is the solution of the equation $x = \frac{1}{6} * x^5 + \frac{1}{3}$. This is because termination is obtained either by choosing (as a first choice) the first implementation (with probability $\frac{1}{6}$) and then having the sub-flow rooted at each of the 5 activities in this implementation terminate (the probability of the latter event is $x^5$), or by choosing the implementation with single atomic activity (and thus terminating). The obtained polynomial is known not to have any rational roots. □

Results by Etessami and Yannakakis [2009] on the hardness of approximating the termination probability in RMCs can similarly be used to show that a PTIME approximation algorithm is unlikely to exist also in our context. Namely, we have the following.

**Theorem 3.36**   The existence of a PTIME algorithm for APPROX-BOOL-EVAL, even for queries with no transitive nodes and edges, implies that $SQRT-SUM \in PTIME$.

SQRT-SUM is the problem of deciding, given natural numbers $(d_1, ..., d_n)$ and a natural number $k$, whether $\sum_{i=1,...,n} \sqrt{d_i} \leq k$, strongly believed not be solvable in PTIME under Turing Computation Model [Garey et al., 1976]. The proof follows immediately from Theorem 12 in Etessami and Yannakakis [2009].

We next show, however, that an EXPTIME approximation is possible, thus proving correctness of the following theorem.

**Theorem 3.37**   For every natural number $j$, we can solve APPROX-BOOL-EVAL, approximating the probability up to $j$ bits of precision, in time exponential in the size of $s$ and linear in $j$.

We will provide a constructive proof of the theorem, by suggesting an algorithm. Our algorithm combines techniques from query evaluation over probabilistic XML [Kimelfeld and Sagiv, 2007] and termination analysis in RMCs [Etessami and Yannakakis, 2009]. We note that the problem here is more complex than the case of XML due to (1) the recursive nature of BPs and (2) the fact that the same specification DAG may be used in multiple places in the execution. These will be reflected by the higher computational complexity. The problem is also more complex than the case of RMCs since on the one hand we need to consider general boolean queries (as opposed to just termination/reachability queries), but on the other hand avoid using general MSO query evaluation techniques since they incur non-elementary query complexity. This will be reflected by the intricacy of the algorithm.

We present the algorithm in two steps. We first consider a restricted setting where the BP specification is non-recursive, and show that *exact* probability computation is possible here (though may be expensive). Then, we explain why this algorithm does not apply to the general case, and show the changes required to obtain an approximation algorithm for this setting.

## 3.5.1    THE NON-RECURSIVE CASE

Even in the absence of recursion, still, an obstacle here, absent from the XML setting, is that the same specification DAG may be used in multiple places of the execution (e.g., as implementation of multiple occurrences of the same compound activity). This increases the algorithm complexity, relative to the XML case.

Our algorithm is based on the following two principles.

**1. Decomposition into smaller problems:** Recall that when a pattern $p$ is embedded into an EX-flow $e$, parts of the pattern are matched to parts of the EX-flow. Our algorithm will correspondingly compute the likelihood of the full boolean query (w.r.t. the given BP) out of the likelihoods of the query parts (w.r.t. parts of the BP). To make this precise we next extend the notions of *queries* and *likelihood*.

a.  Given a query $p$, we denote by $Parts(p)$ the set of all boolean (sub)queries obtained from $p$ by removing one or more nodes and edges, and conjunctions obtained from every subset of these queries. The semantics of a conjunction is the standard one: a conjunction of queries is satisfied by a given EX-flow if there is an embedding of each of the queries in the flow.

b.  Recall that a query (EX-pattern) may include *simple* and *transitive* activities. Implementations of simple pattern activities are matched to *direct implementations* of the corresponding EX-flow activities; implementations of transitive pattern activities may be matched anywhere (deeper) in the implementation subgraph. We extend, correspondingly, our definition of $Parts(p)$: each query $q$ appears in it in two forms: as $q^{direct}$ and as $q^{indirect}$.

c.  We have defined $likelihood^b(p)$ for the likelihood that an EX-flow starting from the BP *root* satisfies the EX-pattern $p$. In an analogous way, for a compound activity $a$ and some $q^{direct}$ ($q^{indirect}$) in $Parts(p)$, we can define $likelihood^b(q^{direct}, a)$ (resp. $likelihood^b(q^{indirect}, a)$) for the likelihood that a sub-flow starting from an implementation of $a$ satisfies $q$ (in)directly. For that, we extend the definition of f-likelihood to sub-flows rooted at any compound activity $a$.

**2. The Principle of Inclusion and Exclusion:** As explained above, our algorithm will compute the likelihood of the full query $p$ out of the likelihoods of other "smaller" sub-queries in $Parts(p)$. In various points of the computation we shall utilize the *principle of inclusion and exclusion* (in its probabilistic form) [Borges, 1973]. This principle allows to compute the likelihood of a disjunction of query parts from the likelihoods of conjunctions of query parts, namely from the likelihood of other sub-queries in $Parts(p)$. Observe, however, that applying this principle yields an exponential blow-up of the size of the expression. Thus, we shall take caution in applying it only over disjunctions whose size is bounded and independent of the BP specification size.

**Algorithm for non-recursive BPs.** We next describe our algorithm, called EVAL-BOOL-QUERY. Without loss of generality we assume below that the query root activity is labeled either by the name of the BP root activity or by *any*. (Otherwise, $likelihood^b(p) = 0$.)

Our algorithm is based on the following intuition. Recall that when a pattern $p$ is embedded into an EX-flow $e$, parts of the pattern are matched to parts of the EX-flow. Our algorithm will correspondingly compute the likelihood of the full answer (w.r.t. the given BP) as an arithmetic combination of the likelihoods of its parts (w.r.t. parts of the BP).

To that end, we denote by $Parts(p)$ the set of all boolean (sub)queries obtained from an EX-pattern $p$ by removing one or more nodes and edges, and all the conjunctions of such queries. The semantics of a conjunction is defined in a natural manner. Further recall that a query (EX-pattern) may include *simple* and *transitive* activities, where implementations of simple (transitive) pattern activities are matched to *direct (possibly indirect) implementations* of the corresponding EX-flow activities. We extend, correspondingly, our definition of $Parts(p)$: each query $q$ appears in it in two forms: as $q^{direct}$ and as $q^{indirect}$. Finally, we have defined above $likelihood^b(p)$ for the likelihood that an EX-flow starting from the BP *root* satisfies the EX-pattern $p$; we can define $likelihood^b(q^{direct}, a)$ (resp. $likelihood^b(q^{indirect}, a)$) for the likelihood that a sub-flow starting from an implementation of $a$ satisfies $q$ (in)directly, by extending the definition of f–likelihood .

Given a query $p$ and a BP $s$, EVAL-BOOL-QUERY (Algorithm 6) computes $likelihood^b(p)$ via Dynamic Programming. Observe that the non-recursive nature of the BP specification induces a *partial order* $>_s$ over its compound activities, such that $a_1 >_s a_2$ if $a_2$ may appear in an EX-flow originating from $a_1$. The algorithm first completes this partial order to a total one (line 1) and processes the compound activities of $s$, in reversed order, from the most internal activities to the root activity (lines 2-3). EVAL-BOOL-QUERY (gradually) fills in a table $T$ of likelihoods whose rows and columns correspond to sub-queries (direct and indirect) and compound activities, resp. For each compound activity $a$ and for all direct (resp. indirect) queries $q^{direct}$ ($q^{indirect}$) in $Parts(p)$, the algorithm computes $likelihood^b(q^{direct}, a)$ ( $likelihood^b(q^{indirect}, a)$), using the likelihoods computed for the preceding activities (lines 5 and 8, resp.). The indirect likelihoods are computed only as auxiliaries, as will be explained below.

Let $\hat{p}$ denote the query pattern $p$ with its root activity removed, and annotated as *indirect*, if $p$'s root activity is transitive, and otherwise as *direct*. Note that with the notations introduced above, $likelihood^b(p) = likelihood^b(\hat{p}, r)$, with $r$ being the root activity of the BP $s$. At the last iteration of EVAL-BOOL-QUERY the root activity $r$ is reached, and (among others) $likelihood^b(\hat{p}, r)$ is computed. Then $T[\hat{p}, r]$, which contains this value, is returned (line 11).

We next explain the two functions responsible for the computation of likelihoods, namely ComputeDirectLikelihood and ComputeIndirectLikelihood invoked in lines 5 and 8 (resp.) of Algorithm 6.

**ComputeDirectLikelihood.** Given $q^{direct} \in Parts(p)$ and a compound activity $a$ of $s$, ComputeDirectLikelihood computes $likelihood^b(q^{direct}, a)$. Recall that $q$ has a nested-DAG shape. The "upper level" of $q$ refers to the outer most nodes and edges of $q$, reachable by paths that do not include implementation edges. A matching of $q^{direct}$ corresponds to (1) matching its upper level to some direct implementation of $a$, and then (2) matching the implementations of the compound

---

**Input:** $p, s$ (with root activity $r$)
**Output:** $likelihood^b(p)$

**1** $activities \leftarrow OrderActsBottomUp(s)$ ;

**2 while** $activities \neq \phi$ **do**

**3**      $a \leftarrow pop(activities)$ ;

**4**      **foreach** $q^{direct} \in Parts(p)$ **do**

**5**          $T[q^{direct}, a] \leftarrow$
         $ComputeDirectLikelihood(q^{direct}, a)$ ;

**6**      **end**

**7**      **foreach** $q^{indirect} \in Parts(p)$ **do**

**8**          $T[q^{indirect}, a] \leftarrow$
         $ComputeIndirectLikelihood(q^{indirect}, a)$
         ;

**9**      **end**

**10 end**

**11 return** $T[\hat{p}, r]$ ;

**Algorithm 6:** EVAL-BOOL-QUERY

---

activities nodes $N_1, ..., N_k$ appearing in the upper level to implementations of the corresponding BP activities (a direct/indirect match for the simple/transitive compound activities).

Ignore for now the matching of the upper level, and consider the compound activities nodes $N_1, ..., N_k$. We denote the sub-queries rooted at these nodes by $q_1, ..., q_k$. If $N_i$ *is transitive, then* $q_i$ *appears in an "indirect" form, otherwise in a "direct" form.* We then consider the matching of all sub-queries, i.e., $\bigwedge_{i=1,...,k} q_i$.

The following identity holds:

$$likelihood^b(\bigwedge_{i=1,...,k} q_i, a) = $$

$$1 - likelihood^b(\bigvee_{i=1,...,k} \neg q_i, a) . \quad (3.1)$$

We thus focus on computing $likelihood^b(\bigvee_{i=1,...,k} \neg q_i, a)$. Using the principle of inclusion and exclusion, this term can be represented as sum of terms, all having the form $likelihood^b(\bigwedge_{i \in J} \neg q_i, a)$ where $J$ is a subset of $\{1, ..., n\}$. Note that the exponential blow-up here is only in the size of the query, and not in that of the BP specification.

Now, re-consider the possible embeddings of the query's upper level, denoted $embs(q, imp)$ for each implementation $imp$ of $a$. Each such conjunction must hold (1) in the chosen implementation of $a$ and (2) for *all* embeddings of the query within the chosen implementation. As we require that for all embeddings, all nodes are *not* matched, we may simply consider a single set of specification nodes, that contain all nodes that participated in any embedding. Moreover, the fulfillment of the negated expression is independent in-between nodes. Thus, we conclude (recall that for a node $n$ of a BP specification, $\lambda(n)$ is the activity name labeling $n$):

$$likelihood^b(\bigwedge_{i \in J} \neg q_i, a) = \sum_{imp \in \tau(a)} \text{c–likelihood}\,(imp) * \prod_{n \in emb \in embs(q, imp)} likelihood^b(\bigwedge_{i \in J} \neg q_i, \lambda(n))$$

$$(3.2)$$

Note that now each of the expressions $likelihood^b(\bigwedge_{i \in J} \neg q_i, \lambda(n))$ satisfies $\lambda(n) <_s a$, as all of these nodes appeared in implementations of $a$. However, $\bigwedge_{i \in J} \neg q_i$ does not belong to $Parts(q)$, so they do not appear in $T$. We thus apply the following manipulation over it. First, we apply negation:

$$likelihood^b(\bigwedge_{i \in J} \neg q_i, \lambda(n)) = 1 - likelihood^b(\bigvee_{i \in J} q_i, \lambda(n))). \quad (3.3)$$

Now we apply again the principle of inclusion and exclusion over $\bigvee_{i \in J} q_i$ (again, only dependent on the query size) and obtain expressions of the form $likelihood^b(\bigwedge_{i \in J'} q_i, \lambda(n))$. The expressions of the sort $\bigwedge_{i \in J'} q_i$ are conjunctions of sub-queries, hence belong to $Parts(p)$, and thus the required likelihood values already appear in the Dynamic Programming table $T$ and can be used.

**ComputeIndirectLikelihood.** The computation here is similar, but slightly more complicated due to the possibly indirect matches. Recall that when embedding a query indirectly, query parts may be matched to different levels of the implementation nesting. Thus, instead of dividing the query simply by its compound nodes, we define the notion of *query splits*. $\{q_1, ..., q_m\}$ is a split of $q^{indirect}$ if each $q_i$ is a sub-graph of $q^{indirect}$, and every node or edge of $q^{indirect}$ appear in exactly one of the $q_i$'s. We denote the set of all splits of $q^{indirect}$ by $splits(q^{indirect})$, and consider the likelihood of $\bigvee_{sp \in splits(q^{indirect})} \bigwedge_{q_i \in sp} q_i$.

By applying the principle of inclusion and exclusion, we obtain expressions of the form $\bigwedge_{sp \in SP} \bigwedge_{q_i \in sp} q_i$ for some subsets $SP$ of $splits$. (Note that the number of splits is, once again, only a function of the query size). We can now unite the two $\bigwedge$ expressions and obtain $\bigwedge_{q_i \in sp'} q_i$ for some $sp'$. From this point on the computation proceeds exactly as for `ComputeDirectLikelihood` (with the only difference being that the $q_i$'s are now not necessarily partial flows rooted at compound activities).

We have assumed above, for simplicity, that compound activities in the query are not annotated by formulas. In the presence of such formulas, the sub-queries $q_i$ in Eq. 3.1 are annotated by the formula of their respective compound activity $N_i$. Then, only implementations guarded by the same formula are considered for embedding (see Eq. 3.2).

**Example 3.38**    To illustrate the operation of the algorithm, let us consider the BP specification $s$ given in Figure 2.5 and the boolean query $p$ of Figure 3.5(a). The BP in Figure 2.5 is recursive, whereas our current algorithm handles only non-recursive BPs. So, just for this example, let

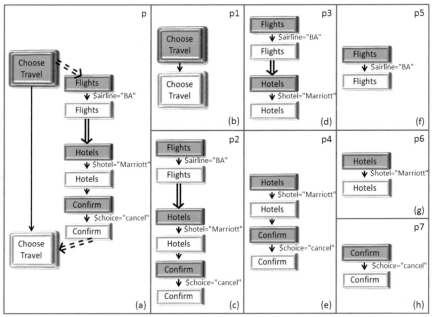

**Figure 3.5:** A Boolean query and its possible splits.

us modify the BP, and obtain a non-recursive one, by removing the implementation guarded by $choice = "reset"$. To compensate for its likelihood, assign a likelihood of 0.8 to the formula $choice = "confirm"$. The activities may now be partially ordered according to the implementation relation, e.g., chooseTravel $>_s$ Login, chooseTravel $>_s$ Flights, chooseTravel $>_s$ Advertise, etc., and this partial order can be completed to a total one. We next explain the manner in which our algorithm computes the $likelihood^b(p, s)$. The computation starts at the "smallest" (according to the above order) activities of $s$, e.g., Hotels, Flights and Confirm. For each such activity, all $Parts(p)$ are matched. Here, most matches yield a match likelihood of 0, apart from those matching the choice of "BA," "Marriott" and "cancel" to the corresponding implementation of Flights, Hotels and Confirm, resp. (yielding likelihood values of 0.7, 0.6 and 0.2 resp.). Proceeding to chooseTravel, we again consider the matching of all elements of $Parts(p)$. In particular, let us focus on the matching of $p2^{indirect}$ to chooseTravel (recall that its likelihood = $likelihood^b(p)$). As we are dealing with an indirect match, we consider all the possible splits of $p2$. One possible split consists of $p5$, $p6$ and $p7$, another consists of $p5$ and $p4$, etc. We disjunct over all splits, and in each split conjunct over all its parts. Observe that the existence of matchings to the splits are *dependent*: for instance, if there exists a match in a given EX-flow to $p5$ and $p4$, then obviously matches to $p5$, $p6$ and $p7$ exist as well. This is where the Principle of Inclusion and Exclusion over all possible splits (along with the likelihood of match for each split) comes into play, for each possible implementation of chooseTravel. At the end of the computation we obtain the following equation:

$$likelihood^b(p2^{indirect}, \texttt{chooseTravel}) =$$
$$\texttt{c-likelihood (\$searchType="flights + hotels")}$$
$$* [likelihood^b(\$\texttt{airline}=\texttt{"BA}^{''indirect}, \texttt{Flights})$$
$$* likelihood^b(\$\texttt{hotel}=\texttt{"Marriott}^{''indirect}, \texttt{Hotels})$$
$$* likelihood^b(\$\texttt{choice}=\texttt{"cancel}^{''indirect}, \texttt{Confirm})]$$
$$+ \texttt{c-likelihood (}$$
$$\$\texttt{searchType}=\texttt{"flights + hotels + cars")}$$
$$* [\ same\ term\ as\ above\ ]\ . \tag{3.4}$$

Additional summands, summing up to 0 due to absence of embedding, are omitted for brevity[8]. Recall that the likelihood values for the terms that appear in the right-hand side of the above equation were already computed in previous steps, due to the bottom-up computation. We thus obtain

$$likelihood^b(p2^{indirect}, \texttt{chooseTravel}) = 0.25 * 0.7 * 0.6 * 0.2 + 0.25 * 0.7 * 0.6 * 0.2 = 0.042.$$

**Complexity.** The number of arithmetic operations performed by the algorithm is polynomial in the BP size, with the exponent depending on the query size. The number of bits of the computed likelihood values may become, however, exponential in the size of $s$, as indicated by the following theorem.

**Theorem 3.39**   Let $n$ be a natural number. There exists a BP specification $s$ of size $n$ and an EX-pattern $p$ (of a fixed constant size) such that the representation of $likelihood^b(p, s)$ requires exponentially many bits with respect to $n$.

*Proof.* We construct $s$ and $p$ as follows. $s$ has a root DAG with a single compound activity $A_0$, having a single implementation (with c-likelihood 1) containing two compound $A_1$ activities. $A_1$, again has a single implementation (with c-likelihood 1) containing two compound $A_2$ activities, $A_2$'s single implementation contains two $A_3$s, and so on, till $A_n$. $A_2$ that has 2 implementations, each with c-likelihood 0.5. The first (second) implementation consists of a single atomic $a$ ($b$) activity.

Now, consider a boolean query $p$ that tests if an activity $a$ occurred somewhere in the execution. ($p$ has a transitive root activity whose implementation consists of an activity labeled by $a$ and connected to the root activity by transitive implementation edges.) $p$ is satisfied by all the EX-flows of $s$, except the one where the implementation chosen for all the $A_n$ activities is $b$. Thus, $likelihood^b(p, s) = 1 - 0.5^{2^n}$, requiring number of bits that is exponential in $n$.

$\square$

---

[8]When a sub-query in this equation is a guarding formula, it represents the empty sub-query annotated by the corresponding formula as its only constraint.

Nevertheless, we note that if we have a unit-cost RAM model with exact rational arithmetic (i.e., algebraic operations on arbitrary rational numbers can be done in unit time) [Blum et al., 1998], we do not have to worry about the size of the numbers. Consequently,

**Theorem 3.40**    For non-recursive BP specifications, BOOL-EVAL is in EXPTIME under Turing computation model and in PTIME (data complexity) with unit-cost exact rational arithmetic.

## 3.5.2    THE RECURSIVE CASE

To see that Algorithm 6 ( EVAL-BOOL-QUERY) cannot be directly applied on recursive BPs as is, observe that it assumed a *total order* over the BP activity names. Likelihood of queries with respect to a given activity $a$ were computed out of previously computed likelihoods for "smaller" activities. Such order does not exist for recursive BPs. We next explain in details the modifications to Algorithm 6, to account for recursive specifications.

    **Data Structure.** As in Algorithm 6, we maintain a table whose rows and columns correspond to query parts an activity names. But the entries of the table will now include equations on variables of the form $X_{q,a}$ for each [sub-query $q \in Parts(p)$, activity name $a$]. The value that will eventually be computed for these variables will (approximately) capture $likelihood^b(q, a)$.

    **Generating the equations.** The algorithm for generating the equations follows exactly the same structure of Algorithm 1, with two distinctions: first, instead of using a bottom up order on the activities (Line 1 of Algorithm 6), which is now impossible, we choose an arbitrary order. Second, we modify the functions ComputeDirectLikelihood and ComputeIndirectLikelihood, as follow.

    **Refined Computation functions.** The refined ComputeDirectLikelihood function, when applied to a sub-query $q$ and activity $a$, returns an equation whose left-hand side is simply $X_{q,a}$. To compute the right-hand side of the equation, the refined function works exactly as the original one, with one distinction: whenever the computation requires use of some $likelihood^b(q', a')$ value (possibly $[q', a']$ is $[q, a]$ itself), and in the original version would look it up in the table, here we simply use $X_{q,a}$ instead of the value and continue the computation. The result is an expression in these variables. Exactly the same modification is applied to ComputeIndirectLikelihood.

    For each pair $[q, a]$, this process results in a single equation; repeating the computation for all pairs of activities names and sub-queries, the result is a set of polynomial equations. We denote the obtained equations system by $ES[s, p]$ for input specification $s$ and EX-pattern $p$.

    **Solving the equations.** We will show below that the least fixed point (LFP) solution of $ES[s, p]$ with all variables in $[0, 1]$, restricted to $X_{p,r}$ ($r$ is the root activity of $s$), is exactly $likelihood^b(p, s)$. We note that an exact computation of this quantity may in general be impossible, as it again may be irrational. Consequently, the last step of the algorithm is to approximate the LFP solution. Here, we use as a black box the construction of Etessami and Yannakakis [2009] (proof of

Theorem 4.2 there) that uses the existential theory of reals [Canny, 1988] to approximate the LFP solution of an equations set (see discussion on complexity below).

**Example 3.41**    Consider again the BP specification given in Figure 2.5, this time with its recursive invocation of `chooseTravel`, and the boolean query $p$ of Figure 3.5(a). The query likelihood, captured as before by $likelihood^b(p2^{indirect}, \texttt{chooseTravel})$, is now represented by the variable $X_{p2^{indirect},\texttt{chooseTravel}}$. The equation defining the variable has a shape similar to that of Equation 3.4 (with the $likelihood^b$ terms replaced by the corresponding variables) and with an additional term on the right-hand side of the formula, corresponding to the possible match via recursive invocation of `chooseTravel`:

$$+X_{\$\texttt{choice}=\text{"reset"}^{direct},\texttt{Confirm}} * X_{p2^{indirect},\texttt{chooseTravel}}.$$

**Correctness.** The correctness of the algorithm follows the following proposition.

**Proposition 3.42**    *The Least Fixed Point solution of $ES[p]$, with all variables in $[0, 1]$, restricted to $X_{p,r}$ ($r$ is the root activity of $s$), is exactly $likelihood^b(p, s)$.*

**Proof.** To prove the proposition we need to show that a Least Fixed Point (LFP) solution exists and captures the correct likelihood values.

We first note that Etessami and Yannakakis [2009] also uses a set of equations to describe the termination probability of Recursive Markov Chains. An important property of their equations is that all the coefficients in the equations are positive. The consequent monotonicity of the polynomials is then used to prove the existence of an LFP.

In contrast, in our case, the equations may have negative coefficients (due to the use of the inclusion-exclusion principle). Thus, the proof of Etessami and Yannakakis [2009] cannot be directly applied here. Nevertheless, the system is "piece-wise" monotone, in the following sense: consider a "part-of" partial order over the sub queries $q$ of $p$ (including $p$ itself). For each such $q$ and an activity $a$, the computation of $likelihood^b(q, a)$ uses either likelihood values computed for queries that are "smaller" than $q$, or values of the form $likelihood^b(q, b)$ for some activity $b$ (possibly $b = a$). We thus solve the equations for $likelihood^b(q, a)$ in an increasing order of such $q$ (and for all compound activities $a$). Now, terms in the polynomial that correspond to queries smaller than $q$ may be simply replaced by constants (computed in previous iterations). After substitution, the formula contains only variables for some $likelihood^b(q, b)$. It follows from the construction that these variables appear with positive coefficients, as follows: recall the computation performed by Algorithm EVAL-BOOL-QUERY and note that $likelihood^b(q, b) = likelihood^b(\bigwedge_{i=1,...,k} q_i, b)$ (where $k$ is the number of query parts considered in a split) may only appear in our computation as is (i.e., as $likelihood^b(\bigwedge_{i=1,...,k} q_i, b)$) or as the "evolvement" (via mathematical transformations) of an expression of the form $likelihood^b(\bigvee_{i=1,...,k} q, b)$ (i.e., using the algorithm notation, $J = \{1, ..., k\}$). Furthermore, note that in each application of the inclusion and exclusion transformation over the above expression, $likelihood^b(q, b)$ is multiplied by $(-1)^{k+1}$. Now let us track back the creation of this expression by the algorithm: at the last step, it was obtained from $likelihood^b(\bigvee_{i=1,\dots,k} q, b)$ and bears a coefficient of $(-1)^{k+1}$. $likelihood^b(\bigvee_{i=1,\dots,k} q, b)$ itself appears in a negative form, thus we have to multiply by (-1) and obtain a coefficient of $(-1)^{k+2}$. Next, we have multiplied expressions by c-likelihood values of guarding formulas, which are positive and do not change the sign. Next, we again used the principle of inclusion and exclusion, leading to the added factor of $(-1)^{k+1}$ and yielding a current total of $(-1)^{2k+3}$ (multiplied by some positive value) as a coefficient. Our last transformation yields a multiplication by (-1), leading to a total coefficient of $(-1)^{2k+4}$ multiplied by some positive value; $(-1)^{2k+4}$ is positive, hence the coefficient of $likelihood^b(q, b)$ in the obtained equation is also positive. The least fixed point solution for the system may thus be computed in a bottom-up fashion (dictated by the order over query parts) using in each step the algorithm of Etessami and Yannakakis [2009]; this least fixed point solution constitutes the correct probabilities.                                                                                                      □

**Complexity.** The generation of the equation system is a similar computation to that performed in the non-recursive case, and is polynomial in the size of the specification for the same reasons. The number of variables in the resulting system is clearly linear in the BP specification size. Then, we use the black box of Etessami and Yannakakis [2009] to approximate the LFP solution to the equations set. To perform this approximation up to $j$ bits of precision, incurs time exponential in the number of variables (and thus in our case exponential in the BP specification size) and linear in $j$. Consequently, this is the data complexity of our algorithm. Thus, the following theorem holds.

**Theorem 3.43**    APPROX-BOOL-EVAL can be solved in EXPTIME (data complexity).

As for query complexity, observe that the number of variables is exponential in the size of the query and thus the overall complexity of the algorithm is double-exponential in the query size.

## 3.6    EVALUATION OF PROJECTION QUERIES UNDER THE *SUM* SEMANTICS

In this section we study the evaluation of top-k projection queries under the *sum* semantics, a problem we refer to as TOP-K-PROJ-SUM. We will observe that boolean query evaluation algorithms can be used as black boxes in the solution of TOP-K-PROJ-SUM, but that nevertheless the complexity of TOP-K-PROJ-SUM, can in general be harder than that of BOOL-EVAL. Then, we show restricted cases that allow for more efficient query evaluation.

### 3.6.1    GENERAL SETTINGS

We next consider the evaluation of projection queries, for general BP specifications and queries. We highlight the difficulties and explain how to overcome them.

*General Framework.* Given a projection query $q = (p, P)$ and a BP specification $s$, a candidate answer is obtained by some (restricted) embedding $\alpha$ that assigns (1) activity names from $s$ to the *any* labels of $P$, and (2) a sequence of labeled nodes to each transitive edge of $P$. (Obviously, some of these candidate answers are not valid, i.e., have no origin flow in $s$, and will have zero likelihood.) Consider such a candidate query answer $\alpha$. Let $\alpha(p)$ denote the pattern obtained from $p$ (including its non-projected part) by instantiating the *any* nodes and the transitive edges in $P$ according to $\alpha$. The likelihood of $\alpha$ is exactly as the likelihood of $\alpha(p)$, treated as a boolean query. Namely, $likelihood(\alpha, q) = likelihood^b(\alpha(p))$

Thus, in principle one may think of the following algorithm: generate all possible embeddings $\alpha$, then use Algorithm EVAL-BOOL-QUERY from the previous section, to compute $likelihood^b(\alpha(p))$ and consequently $likelihood(\alpha, q)$ for each $\alpha$, and finally return the top-$k$ out of these. This is very similar to the framework employed for XML query evaluation in Kimelfeld and Sagiv [2007]. However, there are two obstacles here, absent from the XML settings: first, the number of possible answers may be infinite, and second, there are cases where $likelihood^b$ values may not be computed exactly. We next consider these two obstacles and explain how we tackle them.

**Obstacle 1: Possibly infinite number of answers.** We re-consider the assignments $\alpha$ used, in our general framework, to generate possible query answers. Recall that the assignments are over (1) *any*-labeled nodes and (2) transitive edges. While the number of combinations for the first case (*any* labels) is bounded by $| s |^{|q|}$, the number of possible paths in a recursive BPs, and consequently the number of path assignments to transitive edges, may be *infinite*. This leads to infinitely many possible projection answers. To bound the number of assignments considered for transitive edges, we use the following "small world" lemma.

**Lemma 3.44**   *Given a BP $s$ and a projection query $q = (p, P)$, there exists a set of top-$k$ answers of $q$ w.r.t. $s$ where in each answer all the paths assigned to transitive edges in $P$ are of length bounded by $| s | * k$.*

Intuitively, the proof follows from the fact that for each answer with a path that involves $i$ recursive invocations, there exists a more likely answer, with a (shorter) path where one of the invocations is eliminated. It thus suffices to consider candidate answers that assign, to the transitive edges of $P$, paths of length $\leq | s | * k$. The formal proof follows.

***Proof.*** The Lemma is shown by induction on $k$. Consider first $k = 1$. Assume that $q$ is embedded by some embedding $\alpha$ in some EX-flow $e$, and let $M$ be a path in $e$ such that a transitive edge $T$ of $q$ is matched to $M$. Further assume that the length of $M$ is greater than the size of $s$. In particular, this means that $M$ contains a recursive invocation of at least one activity $a \in S$, otherwise the length of $M$ may not exceed the total number of nodes in implementation graphs of $S$. We construct an EX-flow $e'$ that is obtained from $e$ by subsequently omitting sub-flow of $e$ that are rooted at recursive invocation of activities: first, we omit the sub-flow rooted at the recursive invocation of $a$. If there still exists a recursive invocation of some activity $a'$ within $P$, we then omit the sub-flow rooted at $a'$, and so forth, until any activity name appears at most once among the remaining nodes of the path $M$. We denote the remaining nodes and edges that originally were in $M$ as $M'$, and observe that $M'$ is still a path (as we only removed connected sub-paths of $M$). Clearly, $e'$ is a flow of $S$, and $f\text{-}likelihood(e') \geq f\text{-}likelihood(e)$ due to the monotonicity of $f\text{-}likelihood$. There exists an embedding $\alpha'$ of $q$ in $e'$, obtained from $\alpha$ by replacing the path $P$ assigned to $T$ by the new path $M'$. The same construction may be employed for each such path $M$, and consequently we obtain the existence of a top-1 answer where each path assigned to $T$ is of length bounded by $|s|$.

For $k > 1$, assume that there exists $k - 1$ results with transitive edges mapped to paths of length bounded by $|s| * (k - 1)$. Consider an embedding that assigns a path $M$ of length greater than $|s| * k$. Then in particular, it contains more than $k$ recursive invocations of compound activities. We may employ the same technique as above to shorten the path into a path $M'$ that contains at most $k$ such recursive invocations. $M'$ does not appear as one of the $k - 1$ results as its length is greater than $|s| * (k - 1)$, but it is better weighed than $M$ due to the monotonicity of $f\text{-}likelihood$, and may thus be used as the $k$'th-best result. □

**Obstacle 2: No exact computation for boolean queries.** We showed cases where an exact algorithm for BOOL-EVAL does not exist. In such cases, we must settle for an algorithm for APPROX-BOOL-EVAL that approximates the $likelihood^b$ values up to a given $\epsilon$. However, we can still utilize such an approximation algorithm for *exact* top-k query evaluation, if the answers have *discrete likelihoods*, as defined next.

**Definition 3.45**   Given a projection query $q$ and a BP specification $s$, we say that the answers of $q$ (w.r.t $s$) have *discrete likelihoods* if there exists some $\epsilon$ such that for each two answers $\alpha, \alpha' \in q(s)$ where $likelihood(\alpha, q) \neq likelihood(\alpha', q)$, we have that $|\, likelihood(\alpha, q) - likelihood(\alpha', q)\, | > \epsilon$. $\epsilon$ is called the *separation factor* of $q$ with respect to $s$.

The following lemma holds.

**Lemma 3.46**   *For a BP $s$ and a query $q$ with separation factor $\epsilon$, a set of top-k answers according to approximated $likelihood^b$ values, up to $\epsilon/2$ precision, is also a set of top-k answers for to the exact $likelihood^b$ values.*

*Proof.* Denote the approximated score of a projection result according to our algorithm by $approx\text{-}likelihood$, and the set of $k$ results having the highest $approx\text{-}likelihood$ by APPROX − TOP − K. Assume, by contradiction, that there exists two results $\alpha, \alpha'$ such that $\alpha \in$ APPROX − TOP − K and $\alpha'$ is not, but $likelihood^b(\alpha') > likelihood^b(\alpha)$. Since $\alpha'$ is not in APPROX − TOP − K, it holds that $approx\text{-}likelihood(\alpha') < approx\text{-}likelihood(\alpha)$, i.e., $approx\text{-}likelihood(\alpha) - approx\text{-}likelihood(\alpha') > 0$. But $likelihood^b(\alpha) - \epsilon/2 < approx\text{-}likelihood(\alpha) < likelihood^b(\alpha) + \epsilon/2$, and similarly for $e'$. Thus, $0 < approx\text{-}likelihood(\alpha) - approx\text{-}likelihood(\alpha') < likelihood^b(\alpha) - likelihood^b(\alpha') + \epsilon$. I.e., $likelihood^b(\alpha') - likelihood^b(\alpha) < \epsilon$. But we've assumed $likelihood^b(\alpha') \neq likelihood^b(\alpha)$. This contradicts the assumption of $\epsilon$ separation factor. □

We now have a simple exact EXPTIME algorithm for TOP-K-PROJ-SUM, as follows.

1. Generate the finite set of candidate answers (see below).

2. For each candidate answer, treat it as a boolean query and compute its approximate *likelihood*[b] value (up to an error of $\epsilon/2$, where $\epsilon$ is the separation factor), using an algorithm for APPROX-BOOL-EVAL.

3. Declare the top-k answers ranked by their approximated likelihood value computed in step (2).

The set of candidate answers generated in step (1) of the above algorithm is based on the assignments to *any*-labeled nodes and to transitive edges of the pattern, as explained earlier. We generate here only assignments for which the paths assigned to transitive edges are of length bounded by $|s| * k$ (there are exponentially many such assignments). It is sufficient to consider only answers that may be generated in this way, following Lemma 3.44.

Following common practice, let $F^L$ be the class of problems solvable in time complexity $F$, when given an oracle solving a problem $L$. We obtain the following.

**Theorem 3.47**

1. If there exists an oracle for BOOL-EVAL, then TOP$-$K$-$ANSWERS $\subseteq EXPTIME^{\text{BOOL-EVAL}}$.

2. If *discrete likelihoods* are guaranteed with respect to the input BP and query, then TOP$-$K$-$ANSWERS $\subseteq EXPTIME^{\text{APPROX-BOOL-EVAL}}$.

In particular, using Algorithm EVAL-BOOL-QUERY as an oracle, we obtain the following corollary.

**Corollary 3.48**    TOP-K-PROJ-SUM *may be solved in EXPTIME, for: (1) non-recursive BP specifications, and (2) recursive BP specifications, when the query has discrete likelihoods w.r.t. the specification.*

We next also show that this is the best that can be achieved, in the general case.

**Theorem 3.49**    TOP-K-PROJ-SUM is $\sharp P$-hard (under Turing computation model) in the size of the BP specification $s$, even for non-recursive specifications and for queries with no transitive nodes.

The proof (that follows) is by reduction from the problem of # SAT, the problem of counting the number of satisfying assignment to a 3NF formula, and uses the DAG shape of the BP graphs to compactly represent all possible variable assignments (and consequently an exponential number of paths must be considered).

***Proof.*** We construct the following reduction from ♯SAT. Given a 3NF formula with C clauses and n variables, $x_1, ..., x_n$, we generate a BP specification $s$ and a query $q$ as follows: the BP root activity r has C implementations, each with c-likelihood of 1/C. Each implementation represents a clause, and has a start-node labeled by an activity S, an end-node labeled by an activity E, and three sub-graphs connecting these two nodes, each corresponding to one literal of the clauses. The first activity in each such subgraph is labeled $X_1$. If $x_1$ appears in the corresponding literal positively (negatively), the node labeled $X_1$ has one outgoing edge, whose target is labeled $T$ ($F$). Otherwise, the node labeled $X_1$ has two outgoing edges, to nodes labeled $T$ and $F$. Each of these nodes has a single outgoing edge to a node labeled by an activity $X_2$, and this node again has one or two outgoing edges, depending if the variable $x_2$ appears in the given literal or not, and so on. (Thus, all other $X_i$'s in the subgraph have two children.) The last $T$- or $F$-labeled activities are the sources of edges whose targets are the end-node labeled by E. The EX-pattern of the query $q$ consists of a root activity labeled r with implementation containing two activities, $S$ and $E$, connected by a transitive edge. The projected part of $q$ consists of all nodes and edges of the EX-pattern. Note that an answer of q with respect to s is a path, and this path uniquely defines a truth assignment A for the variables $x_1, ..., x_n$: $A(x_i) = true$ (= false) if the $X_i$-labeled node is followed in the query answer by a node labeled by $T$ ($F$).

We claim that for any value of k, there exist at least k satisfying assignments to the formula if and only if there are at least k answers to $q$ all having probability 1 (i.e., the top-k answers of q all have a probability of 1). To observe that this hold, note that every path that describes a satisfying assignment appears in all implementations of the root (since each implementation includes all paths that are consistent with the corresponding claus), hence its likelihood is 1. On the other hand, for every path that describes a non-satisfying assignment, there is at least one implementation that does not contain it (corresponding to a non-satisfied clause), thus the likelihood value of such a path is less than 1. □

We note that ♯SAT is not known to be solvable in PTIME under the unit-cost rational arithmetic model. Hence, unlike for `BOOL-EVAL`, the existence of a PTIME solution for `TOP-K-PROJ-SUM` in this model is questionable.

As for query complexity, our algorithm for projection queries evaluation incur no asymptotic overhead with respect to boolean query evaluation; that is, for non-recursive specifications the complexity remains exponential with respect to the query size, and for recursive specifications it remains doubly-exponential.

## 3.6.2 RESTRICTED CASES

The relatively high complexity of our problems in the general case naturally lead us to consider restrictions on the input, that will allow for more efficient evaluation. For boolean queries, we have already observed above that if the BP specification is non-recursive, then boolean queries can be evaluated in polynomial time with respect to the BP specification size. But we have also shown that evaluation of projection queries is unlikely to have a PTIME solution even for the non-recursive case. Nevertheless, we next identify a restriction on the query, that will allow for tractable solutions.

**Definition 3.50**   We say that a projection query $(p, P)$ is path-projection-free if the projected part $P$ includes no transitive edge.

Note that path-projection-free queries may still include transitive edges in the pattern $p$, and then it serves as a restriction on qualifying flows (there must exist a path matching the transitive edge); however, it cannot ask to see these paths as part of the answer. Still, useful queries may be posed.

**Example 3.51**   Re-consider our running example, and consider a query that looks for a British Airways flight, followed by some path of choices (represented by a transitive edge) that ends in the choice of a hotel; the query projected part then includes only the hotel activity. This path-projection-free query asks for hotels that are most likely to be reserved in conjunction with the reservation of a British Airways flight.

We then show the following theorem.

**Theorem 3.52**   For path-projection-free queries, Theorem 3.47 holds, with the EXPTIME complexity class replaced by PTIME (data complexity).

*Proof.* We revisit our algorithm for projection queries evaluation and recall that it consisted of two steps: in the first step possible assignments were generated and in the second step their probabilities were computed using our algorithm for boolean query evaluation. The exponential overhead incurred by the computation (with respect to boolean query evaluation) was due to the exponentially many assignments that were considered.

In turn, exponentially many assignments needed to be considered only due to assignments to transitive edges. For queries that do not project over such edges, we do not need to consider these assignments, and instead we can keep the transitive edge in the pattern that is fed as input to the boolean query evaluation algorithm. Consequently, it only remains to consider assignments to *Any*-labeled nodes, whose number is only exponential in the query size but polynomial in the specification size. $\square$

Finally, recall (Theorem 3.40) that if the BP specification is non-recursive, then boolean query evaluation can also be performed in PTIME. Consequently, the following corollary holds.

**Corollary 3.53**   *For non-recursive BP specifications, and path-projection-free queries,* TOP-K-PROJ-SUM *may be solved in PTIME (data complexity) with unit-cost rational arithmetic.*

### 3.6.3 SAMPLING BASED APPROXIMATION

So far in this section we have focused on an "analytical" approach for analysis. An alternative approach that one may consider in the probabilistic setting is based on *sampling*. To conclude this section we thus consider a sampling-based approach and highlight some of its features as well as its limitations in our context. We will consider sampling algorithms for boolean queries; as explained above, an algorithm for (approximate) evaluation of boolean queries can then be used as a black box in the evaluation of projection queries.

**A simple sampling algorithm.** Consider the following simple algorithm SAMPLE that is given as input a BP specification $s$ and a boolean query $q$. Each sample is generated by "executing" the Business Process until termination, i.e., starting from the root of $s$ and repeatedly choosing implementations for unexpanded compound activities, until no such activities remain, meaning that we have a full EX-flow $e$ of $s$ in hand. At each step the implementation is chosen randomly, with probability dictated by the c-likelihood function. The algorithm then evaluates the boolean query $q$ against the flow $e$, checking whether or not there exists a match. The algorithm keeps count of the number of samples $Y$ that yielded a match, and after some fixed number of samples $N$, halts and outputs $\frac{Y}{N}$.

This is a standard sampling algorithm, and we can thus use standard bounds on the number of samples that are required for obtaining a good approximation (with high probability):

**Theorem 3.54** The probability computed by the sampling algorithm converges (as the number of samples grows) to $likelihood^b(s, q)$. The number of samples required for approximating $likelihood^b(s, q)$ up to an additive error of $\epsilon$, with probability at least $\delta$, is $\theta(\frac{ln(\frac{1}{\delta})}{\epsilon^2})$.

**Proof.** To bound the number of samples required for an $\epsilon, \delta$-approximation we use the Chernoff bound. Denoting by $x$ the random boolean variable whose value indicates query satisfaction or dissatisfaction, the output *prob* of our algorithm is the average of $m$ samples of $x$. Denote by $\hat{prob}$ the correct probability of $x$ (the query probability), the (additive) Chernoff bound gives $Pr(|prob - \hat{prob}| \geq \epsilon) \leq 2 * e^{-2*\epsilon^2*m}$ where $m$ is the number of samples. So choosing $m$ such that $-2 * \epsilon^2 * m \leq \frac{ln(\delta)}{2}$, i.e., $m \geq \frac{ln(\frac{1}{\delta})}{4*\epsilon^2}$ is sufficient. □

While the bound on the number of required samples is good, there is an inherent difficulty in employing the suggested sampling algorithm, as follows. Note that the generation of each individual sample involves generating a random full EX-flow of the process by repeatedly and randomly choosing implementations for compound activities, until termination. Unfortunately, this generation may in general fail to terminate. First, there are business process specifications for which this generation has probability 0 to terminate - these are specifications that admit no full EX-flow (e.g., a specification with no atomic activity). This simple example can be identified and discarded in advance; but even more interestingly, we can easily devise specifications for which the sampling algorithm has non-zero but arbitrarily low probability to terminate, as indicated by the following theorem.

**Theorem 3.55**    For every real number $r > 0$ there exists a BP specification $s$ (whose number of activities is independent of $r$) such that the probability $prob$ that algorithm SAMPLE terminates when invoked with $s$ and any boolean query as input, satisfies $r > prob > 0$.

*Proof.* Let $r$ be a real number and let $s$ be a BP specification with root $A$ that has two possible implementations: the first is a chain of two nodes labeled $A$, and the second consists of a single node, labeled with an atomic activity $a$. Denote by $c$ the c-likelihood for the first implementation. Then we obtain that the probability $prob'$ of termination of a single sample is the least solution to the equation $x = (1 - c) + c * x^2$ which can be computed as $\frac{1-sqrt(1-4*c*(1-c))}{c^2}$. This is a continuous function in $c$ and thus its limit as $c$ approaches 1, is its value for $c = 1$, namely 0. Consequently, there exists a choice of $c$ that lead to a solution $r > prob' > 0$ for every value of $r$. The termination of $N$ samples then has probability $prob = prob'^N$ thus $r > prob' > prob > 0$ as required.    □

**The non-recursive case.** Non-termination of the sampling algorithm may only occur in the recursive case, since in absence of recursion any sequence of implementation choices will eventually result in a full EX-flow. However, it may still be very inefficient in some cases. For non-recursive BP specifications, every sample generated by Algorithm SAMPLE incurs generation time that is at most exponential in the specification size (with the basis of the exponent dependent on the specification size as well), since at most a single implementation is chosen for each activity name in a given EX-flow. This bound is tight, i.e., there exists a class of specifications for which the generation of a sample incurs (with probability 1) time exponential in the specification size. To observe that this is correct consider, for every $n$, a specification where the root activity $a_1$ has a single implementation with $n$ nodes labeled with activity name $a_2$, then $a_2$ has a single implementation with $n$ nodes labeled with activity name $a_3$ etc. until $a_n$ which is atomic. The single EX-flow of this specification contains exponentially many implementations.

While the theoretical bounds do not support the use of a sampling based solution, it remains to be checked experimentally whether better performance is obtained in some practical cases.

## 3.7   CONCLUSION AND OPEN ISSUES

To conclude, we list several research directions and open questions in the context of querying business processes. In particular, returning to the desiderata detailed in the beginning of this chapter, we observe that BPQL answers some of these desiderata (declarativeness, different levels of granularity, different types of queries, efficient algorithms for most cases), yet there are still much more to be achieved, including the following.

- BPQL focuses mostly on flow and only model data in a high level. In contrast, languages such as LTL-FO that do allow for query flow-and-data do not allow for a graphical representation, "database-style" selection and projection queries, etc. Having a unified query language that enjoys the advantages of both worlds is an intriguing future research.

• One specifically important benefit of declarative query languages is a seamless optimization. The development of dedicated optimization techniques for the analysis of business processes is an important challenge.

• In addition to selection, projection and boolean queries, it would be interesting to consider the evaluation of other kinds of queries that are analogous to "classic" database queries, in particular queries that involve joins, based, e.g., on activities names or even on data values.

CHAPTER 4

# Other Issues

This book focused in this book on modeling business processes, and the analysis of their possible future executions. In this chapter, we briefly consider two complementary additional issues that are relevant in this context: the design, or mining, of BP specifications, and the analysis of *past executions* stored in logs. An in-depth discussion of these two issues is beyond the scope of this book; instead, we only briefly overview some central aspects in this respect, and refer the reader to previous literature for details.

## 4.1 DESIGNING/MINING BP SPECIFICATIONS

Ideally, a declarative model of the BP specification is designed as part of the process specification, with the actual software that implements the process being automatically generated following the specification (and thus matching precisely the model). In this case, the challenge lies in suggesting effective specification tools, and in particular convenient visual interfaces for the designer. Alternatively, the process model can be defined manually, describing as close as possible the (already existing) BP, or be automatically mined from the available execution logs.

In recent years there has been significant effort in all these directions, in both industry and the academia. However, here too there is still much to be desired. We next review the state-of-the-art in these directions: we first consider manual model design, and then automatic mining tools.

### 4.1.1 (MANUAL) INSTANCE DESIGN

The increasing interest in high-level BP specifications has triggered research and development geared towards *User Interfaces* that will allow such process design. Many of these interfaces are based on process *visualization*. This has many advantages: it allows the designer to easily formulate and modify the process logic, allows users to easily understand the process logic and how to use it, and allows analyzers to easily pose analysis tasks. One standard class of such visual interfaces uses *UML (Unified Modeling Language)* [Booch et al., 1999] *state diagrams*. These are essentially StateCharts [Harel, 1987] with standardized notation. Such state diagrams allow to represent the process flow (using hierarchical states), along with the process interaction with its environment and other processes (i.e., events that affect the flow, messages that are emitted by the process during the flow, etc.) guarding the different transitions. While StateCharts (and consequently UML state diagrams) are highly successful as a user-friendly, graphical model for designers of process *flow*, the incorporation of *data* and its *interaction with flow* in this model may be quite intricate. In principal, this can come as part of the description of events actions that guard the transitions. But unlike the case for flow, the UML state diagrams standard does not dictate any syntax for the exact formulation of events and actions, and the common practice is to use "structured English," or high-level programming languages such as C or Java (but not database query languages) for expressing the conditions and actions.

Another standard for specifying business processes that has emerged in the last decade is the *BPEL (Business Process Execution language) standard*. This standard, developed jointly by BEA Systems, IBM, and Microsoft, combines and replaces IBM's WebServices Flow Language (WSFL) and Microsoft's XLANG. It provides an XML-based language to describe, *in a declarative way*, the interface between the participants in a process, as well as the full operational logic of the process and its execution flow. Commercial vendors offer systems that allow to design BPEL specification via a visual interface, using a conceptual, intuitive view of the process as a graph; these designs are automatically converted to BPEL specifications, *and can further be automatically compiled into executable code that implements the described process*. Unlike StateCharts, BPEL specifications do allow some explicit representation of data. However, this representation is mainly geared towards the modeling of the *interaction* of different processes (and more specifically web-services). It includes an XML schema for sent and received data (captured by variables), and an XPath interface for accessing these variables. But it has no explicit modeling of full-fledged database manipulation.

Figure 4.1 depicts an example BPEL specification, edited through a graphical user interface. The specification given here describes the operational logic of a fictive travel agency called "Alpha-Tours" (as may be observed from the property nodes on the upper right-hand side of the figure). Observe that the *control flow* of the agency is captured via a DAG, appearing in the "behavior" tab; also for every activity, the *input data* type required by the activity and the *output data* type that it generates are depicted as nodes in the "Data" tab; these nodes are connected to the corresponding flow activities through unique "data edges." For instance, the input of the "searchTrip" activity is a trip request, and its output ("tripResults") is fed as input to the "reserveTrip" activity, etc.

On the other hand, as mentioned above, there exist various tools for declaratively specifying business processes / web applications flow and underlying data, such as WebML and Web Ratio [Ceri et al., 2002], WAVE [Deutsch et al., 2005], Hilda [Yang et al., 2007], Siena [Cohn et al., 2008], and others. But they do not allow explicit representation of flow, and in particular do not suggest a user-friendly graphical interface for editing and viewing the process specification. *What is desired, and is the subject of an intriguing research is an interface for visualizing both the processes flow and manipulation of data*. Of course, there may be parts of the specification (both in terms of flow and data manipulation) which are complicated and difficult to visualize in a user-friendly form. However, it is still worthwhile to visualize those parts that are simpler, and perhaps suggest simplified "views" on the more complicated part.

## 4.1.2  MINING MODEL INSTANCE

Even the best interface for process design requires a designer that will use it to specify the logic of the process. Works on *process mining* take an orthogonal approach. They attempt to infer the process structure from a set of observed (perhaps partial) executions. Even if we consider only flow,

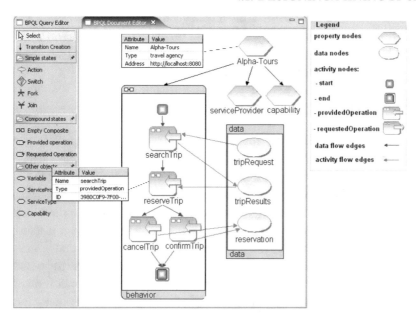

**Figure 4.1:** A process example modeled using BPEL Editor.

this is clearly a challenge: consider a set of logs containing many different operations, occurring in different orders among different logs. Inferring a process model here includes deciding which of these operations are defined to occur in "parallel" (i.e., in an arbitrary order), and which of them are in order. However, it may be the case that for two activities which may actually be parallel in the process specification, there exists some consistent ordering in the given set of logs: simply because the number of "sampled" (observed) logs is not big enough to exhibit all orderings. More generally, identifying the causality relationship between the invocation of activities is a major challenge in this context.

There are several approaches for process mining, attempting to alleviate these difficulties. Some of these approaches use techniques such as neural networks and association rules mining for learning the process structure. This includes the process mining tools in the Business (Process) Intelligence (BPI) suite [Grigori et al., 2004]. While these approaches have experimentally proven successful, it is difficult to provide any formal guarantees on their results. Other approaches [Lary and Young, 1990; Silva et al., 2005] are based on statistics, and try to maximize the likelihood of the observed sequence given the model. These approaches are rooted in works on formal models, such as those on inference of a best fit (i.e., maximizing the likelihood of observations, given the model) Markov Chain [Silva et al., 2005], or a Probabilistic Context Free Grammar [Lary and Young, 1990] for a given set of observations. However, these models typically do not model *parallelism*, which is inherent in process models. Moreover, to the best of our knowledge, these approaches all pertain to the application structure and flow, some of them in the broader context of the organization and the interaction of the process with it and with other processes, *but not the manipulated data.*

**Further reading.** There is vast literature on process mining. We refer the reader to [van der Aalst, 2011] for an overview of the area and recent advancements.

## 4.2   QUERYING PAST EXECUTIONS

We have discussed the analysis of future executions of a given process specification. Equally important is the analysis of executions that took place in the past, and are recorded in a repository. Execution logs are of tremendous importance for companies, since they may reveal *patterns* in the behavior of the users (e.g., "users that book flights of a specific airline also tend to book a specific hotel"), may allow to identify run-time errors that occurred, or a breach of the company policy. In the context of scientific workflows, these execution logs are referred to as *provenance*. They represent instances of the scientific process that was used in practice, and they are in fact the main object that is analyzed in this context. This analysis can verify the correctness of experiments represented by the workflow, identify the different tools that were used, with which parameters, etc. Another application of log analysis is inference of probabilities, based on past observations, for the probabilistic process models discussed in Chapter 2.

### 4.2.1   CONTENTS OF THE LOG

One basic question in this context is what is recorded in execution logs. One option is to record only the execution flow, i.e., the activities (functions, web-services, modules..) that were used at run-time, along with their order of occurrence. But in many cases what is also of interest is the record of *data* that were manipulated/transmitted throughout the execution, and the inter-action of data with the execution flow. This entails "marrying" workflow provenance (that includes record of the activities or modules that occurred at run-time), with the notion of *data* provenance (e.g. [Buneman et al., 2001, 2008; Cheney et al., 2009; Foster et al., 2008; Green et al., 2007a,b; Huang et al., 2008; Vansummeren and Cheney, 2007; Zhou et al., 2010]): the management of fine-grained record on the course of databases queries evaluation.

There are two challenges in this context first, keeping a complete record of all activities that occurred at run-time, and all data that was manipulated, may be infeasible in terms of the *required storage resources.* Second, while parts of the logs may be essential for analysis purposes, it is often the case that other parts of the logs should be kept confidential. How do we decide what to record?

*Fine-grained, flexible Tracing*   There are various works that suggest partial solutions to (different aspects of) this challenge. We have suggested the notion of a *selective tracing* system for BP execution flows, that uses a *renaming function* for activities, to mask the real names of the recorded activities, and a *deletion set* for activities, allowing the deletion of all record of some activities from the execution logs [Deutch and Milo, 2008]. This allows in particular for a flexible granularity and control over what is stored for different parts of the execution. We adapted our notion of queries to account for selective tracing, and showed that in this context the evaluation of selection queries, as well as projection queries under *max* semantics is still feasible (PTIME with respect to the BP specification size) [Deutch and Milo, 2008, 2009b].

In the context of scientific workflows, many works on *workflow provenance* assume that each module is a "black-box," so that each output depends on all inputs (coarse-grained dependencies). Some recent works (e.g., [Acar et al., 2010; Ikeda et al., 2011]) suggest frameworks for keeping track of both the activated modules and their internal manipulation of data. However, the provenance that is tracked there still does not keep track of the exact transformations performed on each data item (in contrast to the case of provenance management in "standard" databases, see, e.g., [Green et al., 2007a]). In contrast, we proposed a framework that "marries" workflow provenance with classic database provenance in a way that allows fine-grained and flexible tracing of executions, while still maintaining a feasibly compact representation [Amsterdamer et al., 2011]. Our framework also allows to choose the desired level of granularity in provenance views and querying, as well as supporting "what-if" workflow analytic queries on the execution logs.

*Privacy Issues*    Davidson et al. [2011] point out that a scientific workflow often contains private or confidential data and uses proprietary modules, that may be revealed as the result of provenance analysis. They distinguish between three types of workflow privacy: *module* privacy, *data* privacy, and *structural* privacy, as follows.

- Module privacy refers to hiding the functionality of one or more modules in a workflow. Module privacy is a very strong notion: for private modules it is required that for any input to the module, a user should not be able to guess with any degree of certainty the module output.

- Data privacy refers to hiding private intermediate data, that is, data flowing between modules in the execution. While the end inputs and outputs of the workflow may be public, intermediate computations may still be kept confidential.

- Structural privacy refers to hiding details of how a particular data item has been generated in an execution, i.e., which modules have manipulated the item.

Work on workflow privacy aims at addressing the tradeoff between the benefit of revealing a lot of information on the workflow executions, for purpose of analysis, and the damage in breaching privacy of the above three flavors. There are still many open challenges in this area [Davidson et al., 2011].

## 4.2.2    FORMALISMS TO USE FOR ANALYSIS

Ideally, the same query language used for querying future executions could be used for querying past executions, with the appropriate adaptation of the query evaluation algorithms. This may allow analysts to only master a single language, allow to combine specification analysis with log querying and allow a uniform development of query optimization techniques. The similarities of solutions entail also similarities in the remaining challenges described above, and in particular the design of a user friendly (graphical) query language, that will allow to query both the flow and data of execution logs. For instance, we have shown that BPQL, originally designed for querying future executions, can be used also as query language for execution logs [Deutch and Milo, 2008]. LTL-FO, mentioned above in the context of querying future executions, can also be adapted for querying past executions. There are also other works (e.g., [Massart et al., 2008]) that show how to use temporal logic for analysis of execution logs.

### 4.2.3    CHALLENGES AND (PARTIAL) SOLUTIONS IN QUERY EVALUATION

One challenge in querying log repositories is that their typical size is very large, as logs are collected over a long period. A first observation is that process logs may be abstractly viewed as graphs that record the execution flow. Much research has been dedicated to query evaluation over graphs, developing various index structures and labeling schemes for the graph nodes to speed up query processing. There is naturally also large body of work on standard database query optimization. But, to our knowledge, the problem of efficient combined analysis of flow-and-data has not yet been addressed.

In the context of business processes, information about the process structure (derived from its specification) may be used to further improve performance. For example, we have developed a framework for type-based optimization of query evaluation on execution logs, based on the observation that the specification reveals useful information on the kinds of flow that can (and cannot) appear in the execution logs, and this information can be used to optimize query evaluation [Deutch and Milo, 2008]. Similarly, Bao et al. [2010] have shown that, using the process specification, one may derive compact labels for the graph nodes, thereby allowing for efficient processing of reachability queries. These works however focus on the flow and extending them to handle data aspects is intriguing.

An additional challenge is that in many cases what is sought for in these logs is vaguely defined as "interesting patterns," and is difficult to express formally. For these reasons, a dominating approach is to use data mining and OLAP techniques for analyzing log repositories. Indeed, many works adapt "classic" data mining techniques such as clustering, association rule mining and various sorts of statistical analysis [Grigori et al., 2004]. One issue that appears uniquely in execution logs (in contrast to "general" data mining) is the *temporal* nature of events. To that end, there are dedicated data mining techniques such as *Sequential Patterns* and *Complex Event Processing* that account for the order in which events occur and find patterns in the sequence of events. But these works focus mainly on the execution flow, rather than on data. Here again what is missing is an effective processing accounting for both flow and data.

### 4.2.4    RUN-TIME MONITORING

To conclude this section we briefly consider a third axis of analysis, namely that of *run-time monitoring* of the process execution. For instance, the owners of the computer store in our running example may be interested in being notified whenever a user places orders for five or more different products in, say, less than 10 s (because this may indicate that a malicious automated process in fact placed these orders).

There have been several approaches to the runtime monitoring of business processes. One approach [Grigori et al., 2004] is to use pre-defined templates (such as a process P was at a state S for more than X seconds), that can be instantiated (i.e., fed with concrete values) by analysts via a form. The instantiated tasks are internally implemented using, e.g., SQL statements. But the templates are fixed and are intended to be designed only by the system administrator, and not by the analyst. This approach is effective in some cases, but fails to satisfy the desiderata we listed above. More in the spirit of our desiderata are works that lift the same formalisms used for static analysis of executions, and use them in the context of monitoring. Specifically, Massart et al. [2008] showed how to use LTL for effective monitoring of distributed systems; this is an interesting direction but it suffers from the same problems discussed above regarding temporal logic. We showed how to adapt BPQL for monitoring tasks [Beeri et al., 2007], but again, the focus is on the process flow rather than its data. As before, we believe that what is missing is a comprehensive flow-and-data monitoring solution, that will preferably be employed uniformly with a solution for the analysis of past and future executions.

## 4.3   CONCLUSION AND OPEN ISSUES

To conclude this chapter, we consider some open questions and promising research directions in this context of the works presented above.

- As in the case with process modeling (and thus not surprisingly), interfaces for designing processes hardly provide tools for modeling the data that are manipulated by the process. Of course, one can design externally a database schema and simply annotate the flow with SQL queries. But still, for instance, visualizing (even some part of) the effect of the data on the flow, and vice versa, is an intriguing and non-trivial task. What is required is an holistic model and visual interface for both flow and data. The lack of treatment of data is even more noticeable in the works on process mining, as observed above; any advance towards this end would be very important.

- The declarative nature of some interfaces for process design, such as BPEL, opens the way for dedicated optimization techniques, improving the performance of the processes. There have been works on optimization of the execution of declaratively described processes, in various contexts (e.g., [Simitsis et al., 2005; Vrhovnik et al., 2007]). However, there is currently no theory of declarative BP optimization that is comparable to the comprehensive theory on database query optimizations.

- Due to the difficulty of process mining, one can consider an hybrid approach, where some parts of (or "clues about") the process specification are given, but other parts need to be inferred from the observed executions. This could model relatively well real-life scenarios.

- We described recent advancements in capturing execution traces and in fine-grained work-flow provenance tracking. More efforts are required to further optimize storage and access to provenance in this context, as well as for the development of further analysis techniques on execution traces.

CHAPTER 5

# Conclusion

This book provided a database perspective to business processes. Research in this area considers the context (processes) in which data are generated and manipulated, the users interacting with the data and the goals that the data serves. We considered different tasks in business process management, including the process *modeling* and its *analysis*. We showed recent advancements in this respect, and provided model definitions and detailed algorithms for analysis under this model.

We argue that similar to the case of "conventional" database research, elegant modeling and rich underlying technology are likely to be the key to successful modeling and analysis, beneficiary to both business process owners and their users. We discussed the state-of-the-art research in this direction and highlighted the remaining gaps.

Due to the limited scope of the book, we could only provide details on a small fraction of works in the area of business Process management, and we focused on a database perspective to modeling and analysis of such processes. Clearly, there are many aspects that were only briefly surveyed; for readers interested in these aspects, references were given throughout the book.

We believe that business processes constitute a very promising area for research. Throughout the article, we outlined our vision for further research in this area. Moreover, we believe that database researchers are best equipped for this research. This is because it seems that the exciting new challenges posed by research in this area may be addressed by careful extension of principles that have led conventional database research: declarative models and languages, accompanied by efficient query evaluation algorithms and optimization techniques.

# Bibliography

S. Abiteboul, R. Hull, and V. Vianu. *Foundations of Databases*. Addison-Wesley, 1995. Cited on page(s) 21

S. Abiteboul, V. Vianu, B. Fordham, and Y. Yesha. Relational transducers for electronic commerce. In *Proc. 17th ACM SIGACT-SIGMOD-SIGART Symp. on Principles of Database Systems*, pages 179–187, 1998. DOI: 10.1145/275487.275507 Cited on page(s) 4, 21

S. Abiteboul, L. Segoufin, and V. Vianu. Static analysis of active xml systems. *ACM Trans. Database Syst.*, 34(4):Article No. 23, 2009. DOI: 10.1145/1620585.1620590 Cited on page(s) 27

S. Abiteboul, P. Bourhis, and V. Vianu. Comparing workflow specification languages: a matter of views. In *Proc. 14th Int. Conf. on Database Theory*, pages 78–89, 2011. DOI: 10.1145/1938551.1938564 Cited on page(s) 4, 5, 21, 22, 23

U. Acar, P. Buneman, J. Cheney, J. Van Den Bussche, N. Kwasnikowska, and S. Vansummeren. A graph model of data and workflow provenance. In *Proceedings of the 2nd conference on Theory and practice of provenance (TaPP)*, pages 8–13, 2010. Cited on page(s) 79

ActiveXml. Active XML, 2003. http://activexml.net/. Cited on page(s) 5, 22, 23

R. Alur, M. Benedikt, K. Etessami, P. Godefroid, T. Reps, and M. Yannakakis. Analysis of recursive state machines. *ACM Trans. Prog. Lang. and Syst.*, 27(4):786–818, 2005. DOI: 10.1145/1075382.1075387 Cited on page(s) 4, 11, 27

Y. Amsterdamer, S. B. Davidson, D. Deutch, T. Milo, J. Stoyanovich, and V. Tannen. Putting lipstick on pig: Enabling database-style workflow provenance. *Proc. VLDB Endowment*, 5(4):346–357, 2011. Cited on page(s) 79

Z. Bao, S. B. Davidson, S. Khanna, and S. Roy. An optimal labeling scheme for workflow provenance using skeleton labels. In *Proc. of SIGMOD*, pages 711–722, 2010. DOI: 10.1145/1807167.1807244 Cited on page(s) 80

C. Beeri, A. Eyal, T. Milo, and A. Pilberg. Monitoring business processes with queries. In *Proc. 33rd Int. Conf. on Very Large Data Bases*, pages 603–614, 2007. Cited on page(s) 2, 3, 5, 9, 13, 26, 28, 81

M. Benedikt, P. Godefroid, and T. Reps. Model checking of unrestricted hierarchical state machines. In *Proc. ICALP*, pages 652–666, 2001. Cited on page(s) 4, 9

M. Benedikt, E. Kharlamov, D. Olteanu, and P. Senellart. Probabilistic XML via Markov chains. *Proc. VLDB Endowment*, 3(1):770–781, 2010. Cited on page(s) 22

L. Blum, F. Cucker, M. Shub, and S. Smale. *Complexity and real computation*. Springer-Verlag, 1998. Cited on page(s) 34, 63

G. Booch, J. Rumbaugh, and I. Jacobson. *The Unified Modeling Language user guide*. Addison Wesley, 1999. Cited on page(s) 75

R. Borges. On the principle of inclusion and exclusion. *Journal Periodica Mathematica Hungarica*, 3 (1-2):149–156, 1973. DOI: 10.1007/BF02018470 Cited on page(s) 57

bpel. Business Process Execution Language for Web Services, 2007. http://www.ibm.com/developerworks/library/ws-bpel/. Cited on page(s) 3, 28

D. Brand and P. Zafiropulo. On communicating finite-state machines. *J. ACM*, 30:323–342, 1983. DOI: 10.1145/322374.322380 Cited on page(s) 9

T. Bultan, J. Su, and X. Fu. Analyzing conversations of web services. *IEEE Internet Computing*, 10 (1):18–25, 2006. DOI: 10.1109/MIC.2006.1 Cited on page(s) 5, 22

P. Buneman, S. Khanna, and W. C. Tan. Why and where: A characterization of data provenance. In *Proc. 8th Int. Conf. on Database Theory*, pages 316–330, 2001. DOI: 10.1007/3-540-44503-X_20 Cited on page(s) 78

P. Buneman, J. Cheney, and S. Vansummeren. On the expressiveness of implicit provenance in query and update languages. *ACM Trans. Database Syst.*, 33(4):Article No. 28, 2008. DOI: 10.1145/1412331.1412340 Cited on page(s) 78

J. R. Burch, E. M. Clarke, K. L. McMillan, D. L. Dill, and L. J. Hwang. Symbolic model checking: 1020 states and beyond. *Information and Control*, 98(2), 1992. DOI: 10.1016/0890-5401(92)90017-A Cited on page(s) 9

O. Burkart and B. Steffen. Model checking for context-free processes. In *Proc. CONCUR*, pages 123–137, 1992. DOI: 10.1007/BFb0084787 Cited on page(s) 9

J. Canny. Some algebraic and geometric computations in PSPACE. In *Proc. of STOC*, pages 460–467, 1988. DOI: 10.1145/62212.62257 Cited on page(s) 64

S. Ceri, P. Fraternali, A. Bongio, M. Brambilla, S. Comai, and M. Matera. *Designing data-intensive Web applications*. Morgan-Kaufmann, 2002. Cited on page(s) 76

J. Cheney, S. Chong, N. Foster, M. I. Seltzer, and S. Vansummeren. Provenance: a future history. In *Proc. 24th ACM SIGPLAN Conf. on Object-Oriented Programming Systems, Languages & Applications*, pages 957–964, 2009. DOI: 10.1145/1639950.1640064 Cited on page(s) 78

D. Cohn, P. Dhoolia, F. Iii, F. Pinel, and J. Vergo. Siena: From powerpoint to web app in 5 minutes. In *Proc. of ICSOC*, 2008. DOI: 10.1007/978-3-540-89652-4_63 Cited on page(s) 76

D. Cohn and R. Hull. Business artifacts: a data-centric approach to modeling business operations and processes. *IEEE Data Eng. Bull.*, 32(3):3–9, 2009. Cited on page(s) 23

B. Courcelle. Recognizable sets of graphs, hypergraphs and relational structures : a survey. In *DLT*, volume 3340 of *LNCS*, 2004. DOI: 10.1007/978-3-540-30550-7_1 Cited on page(s) 12

S. B. Davidson, S. Khanna, S. Roy, J. Stoyanovich, V. Tannen, and Y. Chen. On provenance and privacy. In *Proc. 14th Int. Conf. on Database Theory*, pages 3–10, 2011. DOI: 10.1145/1938551.1938554 Cited on page(s) 79

R. Dechter and J. Pearl. Generalized best-first search strategies and the optimality of A*. *J. ACM*, 32(3):505–536, 1985. DOI: 10.1145/3828.3830 Cited on page(s) 35

D. Deutch and T. Milo. Type inference and type checking for queries on execution traces. In *Proc. 34th Int. Conf. on Very Large Data Bases*, pages 352–363, 2008. DOI: 10.1145/1453856.1453898 Cited on page(s) 3, 25, 44, 78, 79, 80

D. Deutch and T. Milo. Evaluating top-k queries over business processes (short paper). In *Proc. 25th Int. Conf. on Data Engineering*, pages 1195–1198, 2009a. DOI: 10.1109/ICDE.2009.199 Cited on page(s) 3, 53

D. Deutch and T. Milo. Top-k projection queries for probabilistic business processes. In *Proc. 12th Int. Conf. on Database Theory*, pages 239–251, 2009b. DOI: 10.1145/1514894.1514923 Cited on page(s) 3, 53, 79

D. Deutch, T. Milo, N. Polyzotis, and T. Yam. Optimal top-k query evaluation for weighted business processes. In *Proc. 36th Int. Conf. on Very Large Data Bases*, pages 940–951, 2010. Cited on page(s) 3

A. Deutsch, M. Marcus, L. Sui, V. Vianu, and D. Zhou. A verifier for interactive, data-driven web applications. In *Proc. of SIGMOD*, pages 539–550, 2005. DOI: 10.1145/1066157.1066219 Cited on page(s) 2, 5, 22, 27, 28, 76

A. Deutsch, L. Sui, V. Vianu, and D. Zhou. Verification of communicating data-driven web services. In *Proc. 25th ACM SIGACT-SIGMOD-SIGART Symp. on Principles of Database Systems*, 2006. DOI: 10.1145/1142351.1142364 Cited on page(s) 5, 22

A. Deutsch, L. Sui, and V. Vianu. Specification and verification of data-driven web services. In *Proc. 23rd ACM SIGACT-SIGMOD-SIGART Symp. on Principles of Database Systems*, 2004. DOI: 10.1145/1055558.1055571 Cited on page(s) 28

E. A. Emerson. Temporal and modal logic. In J. van Leeuwen, editor, *Handbook of Theoretical Computer Science, Volume B: Formal Models and Semantics*, pages 995–1072. Elsevier, 1990. Cited on page(s) 5, 9, 26, 27

K. Etessami and M. Yannakakis. Algorithmic verification of recursive probabilistic state machines. In *Proc. of TACAS*, pages 253–270, 2005. DOI: 10.1007/978-3-540-31980-1_17 Cited on page(s) 27

K. Etessami and M. Yannakakis. Recursive markov chains, stochastic grammars, and monotone systems of nonlinear equations. *J. ACM*, 56(1):Article No. 1, 2009. DOI: 10.1145/1462153.1462154 Cited on page(s) 12, 55, 56, 63, 64, 65

J. N. Foster, T. J. Green, and V. Tannen. Annotated XML: queries and provenance. In *Proc. 27th ACM SIGACT-SIGMOD-SIGART Symp. on Principles of Database Systems*, pages 271–280, 2008. DOI: 10.1145/1376916.1376954 Cited on page(s) 53, 78

C. Fritz, R. Hull, and J. Su. Automatic construction of simple artifact-based business processes. In *Proc. 12th Int. Conf. on Database Theory*, pages 225–238, 2009. DOI: 10.1145/1514894.1514922 Cited on page(s) 2, 4, 21

W. Gaaloul and C. Godart. Mining workflow recovery from event based logs. In *Proc. Annual Conf. on Business Process Management*, pages 169–185, 2005. DOI: 10.1007/11538394_12 Cited on page(s) 2

M. R. Garey, R. L. Graham, and D. S. Johnson. Some NP-complete geometric problems. In *Proc. of STOC*, pages 10–22, 1976. DOI: 10.1145/800113.803626 Cited on page(s) 56

T. J. Green, G. Karvounarakis, and V. Tannen. Provenance semirings. In *Proc. 26th ACM SIGACT-SIGMOD-SIGART Symp. on Principles of Database Systems*, pages 31–40, 2007a. DOI: 10.1145/1265530.1265535 Cited on page(s) 78, 79

T. J. Green, G. Karvounarakis, Z. Ives, and V. Tannen. Update exchange with mappings and provenance. In *Proc. 33rd Int. Conf. on Very Large Data Bases*, pages 675–686, 2007b. Cited on page(s) 78

D. Grigori, F. Casati, M. Castellanos, M. Sayal, U. Dayal, and M. Shan. Business process intelligence. *Computers in Industry*, 53:321–343, 2004. DOI: 10.1016/j.compind.2003.10.007 Cited on page(s) 2, 6, 77, 80, 81

D. Harel. Statecharts: A visual formalism for complex systems. *Science of Comp. Programming*, 8: 231–274, 1987. DOI: 10.1016/0167-6423(87)90035-9 Cited on page(s) 10, 75

J. E. Hopcroft and J. D. Ullman. *Introduction To Automata Theory, Languages, And Computation*. Addison-Wesley Longman Publishing Co., Inc., 1990. Cited on page(s) 4, 9

J. Huang, T. Chen, A. Doan, and J. F. Naughton. On the provenance of non-answers to queries over extracted data. *Proc. VLDB Endowment*, 1:736–747, 2008. Cited on page(s) 78

R. Hull and J. Su. Tools for composite web services: a short overview. *SIGMOD Rec.*, 34(2):86–95, 2005. DOI: 10.1145/1083784.1083807 Cited on page(s) 4, 21

R. Ikeda, H. Park, and J. Widom. Provenance for generalized map and reduce workflows. In *Proc. CIDR*, pages 273–283, 2011. Cited on page(s) 79

B. Kimelfeld and Y. Sagiv. Matching twigs in probabilistic XML. In *Proc. 33rd Int. Conf. on Very Large Data Bases*, pages 27–38, 2007. Cited on page(s) 56, 66

A. Kucera, J. Esparza, and R. Mayr. Model checking probabilistic pushdown automata. *Logical Methods in Computer Science*, 2(1):12–21, 2006. DOI: 10.2168/LMCS-2(1:2)2006 Cited on page(s) 9

K. Lary and S. J. Young. The estimation of stochastic context-free grammars using the inside-outside algrithm. *Computer, Speech and Language*, 4:35–56, 1990. DOI: 10.1016/0885-2308(90)90022-X Cited on page(s) 12, 77

Z. Manna and A. Pnueli. *The temporal logic of reactive and concurrent systems*. Springer-Verlag, 1992. DOI: 10.1007/978-1-4612-0931-7 Cited on page(s) 9

T. Massart, C. Meuter, and L. V. Begin. On the complexity of partial order trace model checking. *Inf. Proc. Letters*, 106(3):120–126, 2008. DOI: 10.1016/j.ipl.2007.10.013 Cited on page(s) 80, 81

S. P. Meyn and R. L. Tweedie. *Markov Chains and Stochastic Stability*. Springer-Verlag, 1993. Cited on page(s) 12, 18

T. Murata. Petri nets: Properties, analysis and applications. *Proceedings of the IEEE*, 77(4):541–580, 1989. DOI: 10.1109/5.24143 Cited on page(s) 9

Y. Papakonstantinou and V. Vianu. DTD inference for views of xml data. In *Proc. 19th ACM SIGACT-SIGMOD-SIGART Symp. on Principles of Database Systems*, pages 35 – 46, 2000. DOI: 10.1145/335168.335173 Cited on page(s) 45

R. C. Read and R. E. Tarjan. Bounds on backtrack algorithms for listing cycles, paths, and spanning trees. *Networks*, 5:237–252, 1975. Cited on page(s) 43

D. M. Sayal, F. Casati, U. Dayal, and M. Shan. Business Process Cockpit. In *Proc. 28th Int. Conf. on Very Large Data Bases*, pages 880–883, 2002. DOI: 10.1016/B978-155860869-6/50086-X Cited on page(s) 2, 6

P. Senellart and S. Abiteboul. On the complexity of managing probabilistic XML data. In *Proc. 26th ACM SIGACT-SIGMOD-SIGART Symp. on Principles of Database Systems*, pages 283–292, 2007. DOI: 10.1145/1265530.1265570 Cited on page(s) 53

R. Silva, J. Zhang, and J. G. Shanahan. Probabilistic workflow mining. In *Proc. of KDD*, pages 275 – 284, 2005. DOI: 10.1145/1081870.1081903 Cited on page(s) 77

A. Simitsis, P. Vassiliadis, and T. Sellis. State-space optimization of ETL workflows. *IEEE Trans. Knowl. and Data Eng.*, 17:1404–1419, 2005. DOI: 10.1109/TKDE.2005.169 Cited on page(s) 81

M. Spielmann. Verification of relational transducers for electronic commerce. *J. Comp. and System Sci.*, 66:40–65, 2003. DOI: 10.1016/S0022-0000(02)00029-6 Cited on page(s) 4, 21

D. Suciu, D. Olteanu, C. Ré, and C. Koch. *Probabilistic Databases*. Synthesis Lectures on Data Management. Morgan & Claypool Publishers, 2011.
DOI: 10.2200/S00362ED1V01Y201105DTM016 Cited on page(s) 53

W. M. P. van der Aalst. *Process Mining: Discovery, Conformance and Enhancement of Business Processes*. Springer-Verlag, 2011. Cited on page(s) 78

W. M. P. van der Aalst, B. F. van Dongen, J. Herbst, L. Maruster, G. Schimm, and A. J. M. M. Weijters. Workflow mining: a survey of issues and approaches. *Data Knowl. Eng.*, 47(2), 2003.
DOI: 10.1016/S0169-023X(03)00066-1 Cited on page(s) 6

S. Vansummeren and J. Cheney. Recording provenance for sql queries and updates. *IEEE Data Eng. Bull.*, 30(4):29–37, 2007. Cited on page(s) 78

M. Y. Vardi. The complexity of relational query languages. In *Proc. of STOC*, pages 137–146, 1982.
DOI: 10.1145/800070.802186 Cited on page(s) 34

V. Vianu. Automatic verification of database-driven systems: a new frontier. In *Proc. 12th Int. Conf. on Database Theory*, pages 1–13, 2009. DOI: 10.1145/1514894.1514896 Cited on page(s) 4, 21

M. Vrhovnik, H. Schwarz, O. Suhre, B. Mitschang, V. Markl, A. Maier, and T. Kraft. An approach to optimize data processing in business processes. In *Proc. 33rd Int. Conf. on Very Large Data Bases*, pages 615–626, 2007. Cited on page(s) 81

F. Yang, N. Gupta, N. Gerner, X. Qi, A. Demers, J. Gehrke, and J. Shanmugasundaram. A unified platform for data driven web applications with automatic client-server partitioning. In *Proc. 16th Int. World Wide Web Conf.*, pages 341 – 350, 2007. DOI: 10.1145/1242572.1242619 Cited on page(s) 76

W. Zhou, M. Sherr, T. Tao, X. Li, B. T. Loo, and Y. Mao. Efficient querying and maintenance of network provenance at internet-scale. In *Proc. of SIGMOD*, pages 615–626, 2010.
DOI: 10.1145/1807167.1807234 Cited on page(s) 78

# Authors' Biographies

## DANIEL DEUTCH

**Daniel Deutch** is an Assistant Professor in the Computer Science Department of Ben Gurion University. He received his Ph.D. in Computer Science from Tel Aviv University in 2010 and was a Postdoc at the University of Pennsylvania (UPenn), and at the INRIA research institute. His research interests include, among other areas, web data management, data provenance, and inference in database systems. During his Ph.D. studies, Daniel received a number of awards for his research, including the Israeli Ministry of Science Eshkol grant and ICDT best student paper award. Daniel has been a member of the program committee of various international conferences and workshops (including WWW, ICDT, PODS). Daniel's research is funded by grants from the US-Israel Binational Science Foundation and the Israeli Ministry of Science.

## TOVA MILO

**Tova Milo** received her Ph.D. degree in Computer Science from the Hebrew University, Jerusalem, in 1992. After graduating she worked at the INRIA research institute in Paris and at University of Toronto and returned to Israel in 1995, joining the School of Computer Science at Tel Aviv university where she is now a full Professor and Department head. Her research focuses on advanced database applications such as data integration, XML and semi-structured information, Web-based applications and Business Processes, studying both theoretical and practical aspects. Tova served as the Program Chair of several international conferences, including PODS, ICDT, VLDB, XSym, and WebDB. She is a member of the VLDB Endowment and the ICDT executive board and is an editor of TODS, the VLDB Journal, and the Logical Methods in Computer Science Journal. She has received grants from the Israel Science Foundation, the US-Israel Binational Science Foundation, the Israeli and French Ministry of Science, and the European Union. She is a recipient of the 2010 ACM PODS Alberto O. Mendelzon Test-of-Time Award and of the prestigious EU ERC Advanced Investigators grant.

Printed in the United States
by Baker & Taylor Publisher Services